Preface

In today's mobile market, there are several forms of messaging available to customers – instant messaging, SMS (Short Messaging Service) messaging, EMS (Enhanced Messaging Service) and Smart Messaging, to name a few. SMS is the most popular of these messaging services and it is estimated that there will be 100 billion messages sent per month by the end of 2002. The newest evolution in mobile messaging is the Multimedia Messaging Service (MMS). It is as its name suggests the ability to send and receive messages comprising of rich media including text, sounds, images and video to MMS capable handsets. A multimedia message can be a photo or picture postcard annotated with text and/or an audio clip, a synchronized playback of audio, text, and photo or, in the near future, a video emulating a free-running presentation or a video clip. It can also simply be a drawing combined with text. MMS makes it possible for mobile users to send these multimedia messages from MMS-enabled handsets to other mobile users and to e-mail users.

This book details the design and implementation of Short Messaging Service (SMS) and MMS applications. The main aim of this book is to provide SMS/MMS developers with the tools necessary to develop applications which can send SMS/MMS messages to groups of mobile devices.

1. The first section of this book presents a Java SMS application which allows the storage of contacts and groups of contacts. Thus the user of the application can customise his/her own list of contact 'Individuals' and 'Groups' of contacts (Such as: 'Family', 'Friends', 'Work Colleagues' etc). Upon selection of Individual(s) and/or Group(s) a single message such as "how r u all" can be sent to all their respective Mobile Stations (MS) by clicking on the 'Add' and then 'Send' button. The simplicity and ease of use of this application allows a diverse range of users from an individual home user to corporate wide user base. All code is

presented and a working version is freely available for download.

2. The middle section of this book presents a similar group bulk SMS application which is web enabled. The application is written using Active Server Pages and is purely web based. Again, it allows the sending of messages to individuals and groups. For the purpose of sending SMS in each scenario, the Simplewire Active X Software Development Kit is used. All code is presented and a working version is freely available for download.

3. In order for "rich media" MMS messages to be sent and received, they must first be transcoded into the MMS format. Essentially what happens is that the content is tailored before it arrives at the mobile. This tailoring process is called transcoding. Transcoding systems can adapt video, images, audio and text to the individual constraints of different devices. They summarise, translate and convert the content into the MMS format. This section of the book presents a transcoding framework, which enables various rich media files stored on PC to be sent to MMS capable handsets. Transcoding is the area that this project will focus on. A java application is developed that allows a user to select multimedia content stored on the computer and send it to a mobile. The application performs the transcoding of the message content into MMS format and deploys the message to the mobile.

This book is aimed at professional developers and undergraduate university students looking to develop messaging applications in this exciting area of mobile communications. All code for the above working applications is available freely from http://www.infm.ulst.ac.uk/~kevin/sms-mms.htm.

Table of Contents

LIST OF FIGURES

List of Tables

Abbreviations

2G	Second Generation
3G	Third Generation
3GPP	Third Generation Partnership Project
3GPP2	Third Generation Partnership Project 2
ANSI	American National Standards Institute
TIA	Telecommunications Industry Assoc.
EIA	European Information Association
API	Application Programming Interface
AWT	Abstract Window Toolkit
BSC	Base Station Controllers
BTS	Base Transceiver Stations
CDMA	Code Division Multiple Access
CRC	Cyclic Redundancy Check
EMS	Enhanced Messaging Service
ESME	External Short Message Entity
GPS	Global Positioning Systems
GSM	Global System for Mobile Comms
GUI	Graphical User Interface
HCI	Human Computer Interface
HLR	Home Location Register
HTTP	Hypertext Transfer Protocol
IDE	Integrated Development Environment
IDEN	Integrated Digital Enhanced Network
IMEI	International Mobile Equipment Identity
IMSI	International Mobile Subscriber Identity
IP	Internet Protocol
JDK	Java Development Kit
JFC	Java Foundation Class
JRE	Java Runtime Environment
LAN	Local Area Network
MAP	Mobile Application Part
MMS	Multimedia Messaging Service
MS	Mobile Station
MC	Message Center
PC	Personal Computer
PDU	Protocol Data Unit
SDK	Software Development Kit
SIM	Subscriber Identity Module
SM	Short Message
SMPP	Short Message Peer-to-Peer
SME	Short Message Entity
SMS	Short Messaging Service
SMSC	Short Messaging Service Centre

SMTP	Simple Mail Transport Protocol
SNPP	Simple Network Paging Protocol
STP	Single Transfer Point
SS7	Signalling System 7
TCAP	Transactional Capabilities App Part
TDMA	Time Division Multiple Access
UCP	Universal Computer Protocol
UK	United Kingdom
UMS	Unified Messaging Service
VLR	Visitor Location Register
VM	Virtual Machine
WCTP	Wireless Comm. Transport Protocol
WAP	Wireless Application Protocol
WML	Wireless Mark-up Language
WMP	Wireless Messaging Protocol

1 The Short Message Service

The Short Message Service (SMS) is a standard for sending and receiving short, text-based messages, usually between wireless devices such as cell phones and pagers. The text can comprise of words or numbers or an alphanumeric combination. Message lengths vary according to network provider, usually between 100 and 256 characters. SMS can deliver messages any time, regardless of whether data or voice calls are in progress. In Europe, SMS messaging has been popular for some time and is slowly gaining popularity in North America. SMS is a universal data service and is supported on GSM, TDMA, CDMA, iDEN, ANSI/TIA/EIA-41, 3GPP and 3GPP2 networks and topologies. These networks communicate over numerous protocols such as SMPP, UCP, HTTP and SMTP1. SMS is embedded in the GSM communications standard that exists on every continent and incorporates advanced services and features that have made it a model for third-generation cellular systems.

SMS first appeared in Europe in 1991 as part of the GSM Phase 1 standard published in 1990. The first SMS message was sent in December 1992 from a PC to a mobile phone on the Vodafone GSM network in the UK. SMS grew rapidly with GSM as it became the international standard for personal wireless communication. SMS slowly gained popularity in North America as some of the major wireless networks (like AT&T) began to support it [Malhotra01]. Figures released by The Mobile Data Association (MDA) revealed that Person-to-person SMS text messaging for June 2002 stand at 1.3 billion and are up by 380 million on the previous year (see Figure 1). Britons sent 45 million text messages each day across the four UK GSM network operators compared to just over 32 million sent in June 2001 (see Figure 2) [Mobiledata02].

---

1 Refer to previous pages for abbreviations.

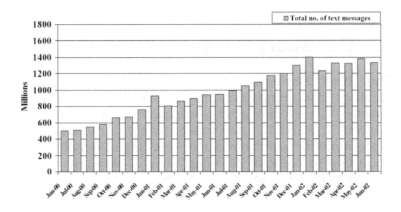

Figure 1: Text Messaging Growth (SMS)

Source: [Mobiledata02].

"Text messaging is continuing to rise in popularity and diversity", comments Mike Short, Chairman of the Mobile Data Association. "As well as person to person text messaging we are seeing interactive text as a popular communication tool. An example of this was the Big Brother 3 interactive voting which seen an increase of 52% (11.03 million), compared to 2001, for the first six weeks of voting, of which 24% were mobile text votes across all networks" [Mobiledata02].

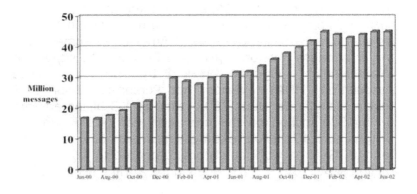

Figure 2: Text Messaging Growth (SMS)

Average Number of Text Messages Sent Per Day in the UK June 2000 – June 2002 [Mobiledata02].

1.1 Benefits and Limitations of SMS

SMS is relatively inexpensive. 160 characters take up as much room as a one-second-voice call [Tull02]. It is also non-bandwidth intensive. Messages are delivered immediately or when the phone is turned on. Like e-mail, text messages can be stored and reviewed at a later date. SMS enables users to send group text messages and it notifies users instantly when a text message has been received.

If the recipient's mobile device is not powered on, the Short Messaging Service Center (SMSC) stores the message and later forwards the message on when the recipient's device is available. It can deliver messages anytime, regardless of whether data or voice calls are in progress and can be easily integrated into Internet based applications or other data applications [Malhotra01]. SMS applications can be programmed using many programming languages, such as Visual Basic, Java, Perl or PHP. In contrast WAP applications must be implemented using WML. A mobile device does not need a browser to receive and send SMS messages unlike WAP. There is also an ability to screen/limit messages and return calls in a selective way – by voice call or by SMS.

The message length however is limited to that allowed by the service provider – usually between 100 and 256 characters therefore it is not suited for long reports. SMS at present does not fully support audio or graphics but progress is being made however with SMS evolving into Enhanced Messaging Service (EMS) and eventually Multimedia Messaging Service (MMS). The store and forward mechanism of SMS, does not make it suitable for WAP applications and the signalling channel used by SMS is used for other purposes, which tends to slow the message transmission rate [Malhotra01].

Application developers have to deal with obstacles such as fragmentation of carriers, inconsistent transport mechanisms and differing message lengths.
A lack of standards for SMS has increased development learning curves and slowed down adoption rates and

different wireless networks deliver SMS and these networks communicate over numerous protocols [Simplewire].

In addition, many service providers do not allow public access or even private access to their networks; this leaves application developers with very few options.

The Protocol Data Unit (PDU), as explained later in the section on Short Message Data Structure, is not flexible with many of the header fields being fixed which can restrict application development.

1.2 SMS Architecture

The two basic elements within SMS networks are Short
Message Entity (SME) and the Message Center (MC) (see
Figure 3). The SME is a device like a mobile phone, or an
application like e-mail (ESME), that is capable of receiving
and sending alphanumeric messages.

Figure 3: Elements of a SMS Network [Hume01].

The MC provides routing and forwarding functions,
including:

- Forwarding messages to the correct SME.
- Storing & forwarding messages for unavailable
  SMEs.
- Applying   originating   and   terminating
  supplementary services such as delayed delivery,
  repeated delivery or distribution list delivery.
- Providing optional internetworking with other
  elements such as a web server [Hume01].

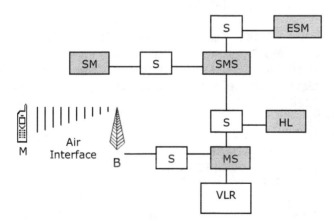

Figure 4: Basic Architecture of a SMS Network

The structure within the MC differs depending on the network and topology used. SMS is offered across multiple networks, the most common being ANSI/TIA/EIA-41, GSM, 3GPP and 3GPP2. The following are descriptions of the SMS architecture elements:

- SIM Subscriber Identity Module, otherwise known as a SIM card. A smart card device that identifies the subscriber. It contains the International Mobile Subscriber Identity (IMSI) and associates it with the wireless device's International Mobile Equipment Identity (IMEI). The SIM card stores SMS messages received until the user deletes them.

- MS Mobile Station, a wireless terminal that is capable of receiving and sending alphanumeric messages. Contains the radio interface as well as the SIM card.

- Air Interface The Air Interface is defined in each one of the different wireless technologies (GSM, ANSI/TIA/EIA-41). These standards specify how the voice or data signals are transferred from the MSC to the handset and back, as well as the utilization of transmission frequencies, considering the available bandwidth and the system's capacity constraints [SMS-Tut02].

- BS Base Station relays information between the MS and the MSC. The BS consists of Controllers, Base Station Controllers (BSC) and Base Transceiver Stations (BTS), also known as "cells."

- STP Single Transfer Point, allows for interconnections over Signalling System 7 (SS7) links and multiple network elements such as X.25 or TCP/IP.

- MSC Mobile Switching Center switches connections between mobile stations, or between mobile stations and the fixed network and performs protocol internetworking.

- VLR Visitor Location Register is the temporary data store in each MSC where information about roaming subscribers is stored. The VLR contacts the subscribers HLR when they roam into its area, and then downloads relevant information needed to offer services to the MS [Hume01].

- HLR Home Location Register is where a given MSs subscriber record and configuration are stored. It defines the MSs network coverage and identifies its boundaries. Also if a message has been transmitted and the destination station was not available when the message delivery was attempted, the HLR informs the SMSC that the station is now recognized by the mobile network to be accessible, and thus the message can be delivered.

- SMSC Short Message Service Center, combination of hardware and software responsible for storing and forwarding messages to and from the MS.

- SME Short Message Entity, which can be a device like a mobile phone, that is capable of receiving and sending alphanumeric messages [Malhotra01].

- ESME External Short Message Entity, is an external application that is capable of receiving and sending alphanumeric messages such as email, voice mail and SMS applications such as the one outlined in this project.

- MAP Mobile Application Part defines the methods and mechanisms of communication in wireless networks and employs the services of the SS7 Transactional Capabilities Application Part (TCAP).

1.3 Short Message Data Structure

A short message is formally known as a Protocol Data Unit (PDU) and is made up of two parts – the header and the message itself (user data). The SMSC identifies the destination of the message by looking at its header information which consists of [2]:

- *SMSC Address* – which the message is to be sent.

- *Destination Address* – of the recipient of the message, specified by the user.

- *Originating Address* – of the sender of the message, automatically set.

- *Status Report Request* – allows sender to request confirmation that the short message has been delivered.

- *Service Center Timestamp* – the time/date the SMSC received the message, automatically set.

- *Validity Period* – sets the maximum time that the message is retained in the SMSC. Failure to successfully deliver the message within this time results in the message being deleted. The user can set the Validity Period, however network operators set default Validity Periods. For example, Vodafone has a validity period of 72 hours.

- *Protocol Identifier* – is a flag that determines how the message should be handled by the receiving device or the SMSC. Some network operators do not support the Protocol Identifier.

- *Replay Path* – allows the user to indicate to the receiver that a reply is requested. The Originating Address of the message is automatically used as the Destination Address. The sending device is

---

[2] http://www.mobiledevelopers.com/smsdevelopers.asp

charged for the reply rather than the replying device.

- *Message Reference* – is assigned by the mobile phone automatically to each message with an identifier modulus 255, which increments with each message sent.

- *Message Length* – is assigned by the mobile phone automatically setting the maximum length of a message. Message Length varies depending on network provider.

- *Reject Duplicates* – allows the sender to indicate to the SMSC to discard duplicate messages.

- *User Data Header Indicator* – enables the sender to specify that the message text itself (user data) is in a special format such as SMS concatenation.

- *SMS Commands* – Some network providers allow the sending device to send specific instructions to the SMSC so as to carry out operations on previously submitted messages. For example, delete a message that is waiting to be delivered.

- *Message Type Indicator* – indicates whether a message is for sending, receiving, is a status report, or a specific command to the SMSC. Automatically set when the message is sent[3].

---

[3] http://www.mobiledevelopers.com/smsdevelopers.asp

1.4 How SMS Works

In this section, we examine the process of sending a SMS message from an ESME to a MS and from a MS to a SME [SMS-Tut02].

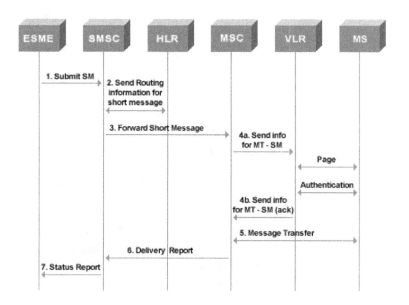

Figure 5: SMS message from an ESME to a MS

MT – Mobile Terminated, SM – Short Message ack – Acknowledge

- The message is submitted from the ESME to the SMSC.
- After completing its internal processing, the SMSC interrogates the HLR and receives the routing information for the mobile subscriber.
- The SMSC sends the message to the MSC using the forward short message operation.
- The MSC retrieves the subscriber information from the VLR. This may include an authentication procedure.
- The MSC transfers the message to the MS via the Air Interface.

- The MSC returns to the SMSC the outcome of the forwarded message.
- If requested by the ESME, the SMSC returns a status report indicating whether or not the message was delivered [SMS-Tut02].

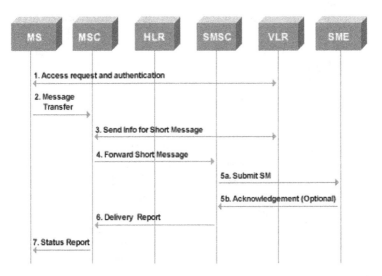

Figure 6: SMS message from a MS to an SME

SM – Short Message

- The MS is turned on and registered with the network.
- The MS transfers the SM to the MSC via the Air interface.
- The MSC interrogates the VLR to verify that the message transfer does not violate the supplementary services invoked or the restrictions imposed.
- The MSC sends the short message to the SMSC using the forward short message operation.
- The SMSC delivers the short message to the SME (and optionally receives acknowledgment).
- The SMSC acknowledges to the MSC that the message was delivered successfully.
- The MSC provides feedback to the MS user that the message was delivered successfully or not [SMS-Tut02].

1.5 Encryption and Security

Security is important for SMS based applications, especially in banking and other sensitive uses such as credit transfer applications. To ensure that short messages do not get corrupted or intercepted, data integrity is incorporated into the networking standard. The SMS message passing across the signalling channel is split into 23 byte segments, each of which is protected by a 5 byte 'fire code', which provides a Cyclic Redundancy Check (CRC). Forward error protection is incorporated using conventional encoding.

All of the information inside and outside of the short message text itself is included in the check. This check is automatically calculated over the Air Interface and between the BS and the SMSC. Short messages are encrypted over the Air Interface using IA5 encryption algorithm. Because of this high level of security, no message has ever been intercepted and read.

1.6 Buyers and Sellers of SMS

The main usage areas for SMS are: Messaging, Mobile commerce, Information services, Entertainment, Customer relationship management, Mobile marketing and Work force management [Northst01]. Sellers of SMS can be divided into 2 main areas: Producers and Resellers of SMS. Producers of SMS own the SMSC, which they use to sell SMS capacity to resellers and users of SMS. Examples of Producers are service providers such as Vodafone. Producers have more control and can offer advanced features like interactivity, alphanumerical sender and user data header. They also have control over the messages being sent and received, by operating their own SMSC, placing them in a good position to guarantee service delivery. Many service providers prefer to sell SMS capacity to resellers rather than users, due to the high cost and hassle of managing business partnerships with other service providers. Without partnerships in place MSs could only send messages to

MSs using the same service provider, thus limiting users [Northst01].

Buyers	Individuals
	Internet portal
	Enterprise
	Application service provider
	Mobile advertising
	Mobile voting
	Mobile portal
	Content provider
	Gateway provider
Sellers	Mobile network operator
	Mobile virtual network operator
	Gateway provider

Table 1: Buyers and Suppliers of SMS

Resellers of SMS do not own an SMSC but access SMS capacity from producers of SMS, by owning and operating an SMS Gateway. Reseller's are middlemen between service providers or owners of SMSC's and users. Their ability to offer advanced features are restricted by the capabilities of the provider's SMSC they access. However, they are more flexible than Producers of SMS as they are able to enter into multiple partnership agreements with multiple service providers in different countries, and offer SMS users the convenience of an international packaged solution at a fixed price and the reliability of multiple routing options arising from access to several providers' SMSCs [Northst01]. An example of a Reseller is Simplewire [Simplewire]. Others include: Noctor[4], Empower Interactive Group[5], and Clickatell[6].

---

[4] http://www.noctor.com/
[5] http://www.eigroup.com/
[6] http://www.clickatell.com/

1.7 SMS User Applications

According to the GSM standard there are two different types of SMS:

1. Point to Point – delivers short text messages from one subscriber to another. Once the message is sent, an acknowledgement of receipt is provided to the sender.
2. Cell Broadcast – permits a number of unacknowledged general messages to be broadcast to all receivers within a particular region or designated cells. Typically used for delivering weather, traffic, advertising or other local information.

SMS applications can implement both types of SMS. SMS applications can be Consumer-based or Commercial/enterprise applications [Malhotra01]. Examples of SMS consumer applications include:

- Peer-to-peer messaging – Most common application of SMS. Simple transfer of messages between users, such as "Football tonight at 7".

- Information services – such as stock quotes, weather forecasts, and news updates. A simple SMS application would require a user to type in "ST" for stock quotes. Upon sending the message to a predefined number, the user would receive the stock quotes in the form of an SMS message [Malhotra 01].

- Advertising – SMS can be used to send targeted alerts to a user. This typifies the ability of SMS to 'push' information onto the user. For example, if the user signs up to his local jeans store. Special alerts could be sent from the jeans store informing the user of the latest stock in his size. Businesses can use SMS as a form of low-cost advertising.

Examples of SMS Commercial/enterprise applications:

- Emergency service – An SMS application could be linked to an emergency alarm device situated in every house. The device could be activated by pressing a button or be connected automatically to the fire and burglary alarm system. It could send vital information quickly to the correct emergency service without the need to ring 999 and explain the circumstances.

- Customer service – SMS can be used as a customer service tool, thereby avoiding expensive person-to-person voice calls.

- Job dispatch – SMS can be used in job dispatching applications to communicate information between office-based and mobile staff. The dispatch application can be integrated with other applications, such as Global Positioning Systems (GPS) [Malhotra 01].

1.8 Developing SMS Applications

SMS applications can be programmed using various languages, including: Java, Visual Basic, Perl, C and ActiveX, etc. Developers of SMS applications have several options:

1. Using an Application Programming Interface (API) made available from a service provider.
2. Using Simple Mail Transport Protocol (SMTP).
3. Using the Mobile Application Part (MAP) directly.
4. Using a Reseller (Third-party) of SMS.

1.8.1 Using a Service Provider API

Service providers (Producers of SMS) are reluctant to allow developers to connect to their SMSC. This is due to the variable costs tied to each message and problems identified previously. In most cases, an account with each provider will be required in order to make an API via TCP/IP available. Some accepted APIs for communicating between the ESME and the providers SMSC include the Simple Network Paging Protocol (SNPP), the Wireless Communication Transport Protocol (WCTP), and the Short Message Peer to Peer (SMPP) [Simplewire]. This method will give users direct access to the advanced features offered by the service provider but may limit them to that individual service provider unless the provider has entered into partnership agreements with other service providers. This method may also restrict the developer into using a protocol or programming language that does not integrate well with the SMS application.

1.8.2 Using SMTP

Most service providers now expose a SMTP, which provides developers with an e-mail interface to send SMS messages. The e-mail address is the devices address, along with the service providers' domain. For example, a message sent to a Sprint phone will have an e-mail address of 123456789123@messaging .sprintpcs.com. Sending SMS via e-mail still has many disadvantages, including speed, assurance, error checking, features, and consistency. Most text messages that are sent through e-mail experience delays ranging from 1 minute to 2 hours. Message lengths greater than that allowed by the service provider will omit those parts of the message that are greater than the maximum allowable length.

The e-mail format does not correspond to the PDU format and will produce inconsistent messages, for example the Subject field may be used as the message text, rather than the Body field. Finally, SMTP does not make available many of the features available with SMS, such as one-touch callback. This method limits your flexibility but is one of the simplest methods to implement [Simplewire].

1.8.3 Using the MAP Directly

This option uses the GSM or ANSI/TIA/EIA-41 MAP directly. This is often used when constructing web-based or API-enabling gateways, WAP gateways, or specialised applications [Hume01].

1.8.4 Using a Reseller (Third-party) of SMS

Using a reseller provides a very simple and efficient mode for sending and receiving SMS [Simplewire] . The reseller usually provides a development kit so that the developers' application can integrate with the resellers Gateway. Some resellers such as Simplewire provide several development kits for different programming languages. This gives the developer a choice of programming languages for implementing the SMS application rather than being restricted to a specific language. The reseller looks after the complexity of routing the text messages to the various service providers SMSCs.

This option is the most flexible method due to its range of programming platforms and its diverse coverage of service providers. However, the inclusion of a third party into the supply chain can push up the cost per text message. Many resellers do not cater for all the different features and functionality offered by the service providers, thus limiting users. Some resellers for example, only offer one-way text messaging.

1.9 SMS Future Developments

SMS is already a mature technology and is the profit generating mobile service. WAP is still early in its technology cycle with low market penetration. GPRS (General Packet Radio Service) also known as 2.5G, is based on a packet-switched wireless protocol is just starting to roll out. The difference between GSM and GPRS, apart from higher transmission speeds, is that GPRS is always on, and the customer is charged based on the amount of data transmitted rather than on the length of time the user is connected to the network. 3G based on UMTS (Universal Mobile Telecommunications System) is even earlier in its technology cycle than GPRS. UMTS will work at higher speeds than GPRS. There are questions regarding the future place of SMS in an environment where technologies such as GPRS and 3G will be available. The answer probably lies in an evolution of the SMS standard in order to take advantage of the increased bandwidth. However, the current strength of SMS guarantees a lifetime for at least the next couple of years before being merged into a more comprehensive messaging solution [Allamaraju01].

The following development technologies are indications of the future evolution of the SMS standard:

Smart Messaging
Nokia developed smart Messaging in 1997 for sending and receiving ring tones, picture messages, operator logos, business cards, calendar requests, and internet settings via SMS[7].

Instant Messaging
Instant Messaging systems enable users to chat instantly online, one such technology is Jabber (http://www.jabber.org). Several efforts are underway to add SMS transport support to Instant Messaging systems. This will allow seamless transmission of data between endpoints regardless of whether they are IP based or wireless based [Hume01].

EMS
EMS evolves from SMS and allows the opportunity to send a combination of simple melodies, pictures, sounds, animations, modified text and standard text. EMS will connect the wireless world to the internet, allowing users to download pictures and ring tones to their phone. EMS works with the existing infrastructure laid down by SMS, as well as utilizing the same familiar user interfaces and remaining compatible with existing mobile devices [Simplewire].

MMS
The next step after EMS is MMS. MMS will depend on the formation of a new faster network infrastructure such as 3G, and will allow users to send messages comprised of a combination of text, sounds, images and video to new MMS enabled MSs. MMS will still have some of the SMS features such as store and forward and confirmation of message delivery but will involve a whole new set of protocols, delivery mechanisms and platforms. We look at MMS in more detail later in the book.

UMS

---

[7] http://www.nokia.com

UMS enables messages of different media such as SMS, e-mail, voice and fax to be accessed from one mailbox. There will be a single common control point for UMS, possibly a PC whereby users can access directly or by using their MMS enabled MSs.

2 An SMS Java Application

This chapter details the development of a Java SMS application using the Java programming language enabling an individual to send batch SMS messages from their personal computer (PC) to a Mobile Station (MS). The source code is given and freely available for non-commercial use.

The SMS application is created using Java based on the Simplewire™ Java SMS Software Development Kit (SDK) [Simplewire]. Simplewire acts as an operating system between the Internet and wireless devices. Simplewire provides three Java classes (Simplewire™ Java SMS SDK), which can be integrated into a Java application enabling it to send text messages to MSs. The user interface is developed using the Java Swing components. A simple form is constructed so that the user can enter

- Mobile number – numeric address of individual(s) MS.
- From text – sets a name for the sender of the message.
- Callback number – sets the senders MS address.
- Message – the SMS body text.

Storage of contacts is accommodated in the interface using a tabbed pane with two tabs, one for 'Individuals' the other for 'Groups'. Both appear alphabetically and have checkbox's next to each contact so that they can be selected and added to the mobile number field. There are four easy steps to sending batch SMS text messages. Users write the text message, click on the contacts or groups they want, 'Add' them to the mobile number field and finally click on the 'Send' button. Contacts can easily be added and deleted by clicking on the 'Add Contact' button, and 'Delete' button respectively. The SMS application is portable as it is programmed using only Java and can be used in a corporate network by placing it on the server, adding employees as 'Individuals', and entering them into corporate sectors such as 'Sales Department', which is then added as a 'Group'.

2.1 SMS Application Requirements

User requirements can be described as the functional requirements necessary for a user to successfully carry out the relevant activities in order to achieve goals while application requirements can be described as the non-functional requirements that are necessary to ensure that the application is both technically and fundamentally sound. To help you, the user achieve these goals the following basic requirements have been identified:

- The application should allow contacts to be stored and viewed in alphabetic order.
- The application should allow groups and group contacts to be stored and viewed in alphabetic order.
- The application should allow the user to send individual or group text messages.
- Send text messages in several ways, by typing the mobile address directly or by selecting contacts from storage.
- Enable the user to delete contacts and groups.
- The application should give the user feedback, for example, an error message stating that a text message was not sent and the reasons why.
- User input must be validated.
- A Graphical User Interface (GUI) that adheres to the Human Computer Interface (HCI) design Guidelines.

With regards to application requirements, several key non-functional requirements have been identified:

- Performance and efficiency – the need for the application to handle storage of contacts in an efficient way and ensure that text messages are delivered quickly with prompt feedback.

- Portability – The application should be platform independent, allowing a user on different computer operating systems or computer architectures to run the application.

- Flexibility – The application should be capable of sending text messages to various groups and groups of individuals simultaneously.

- Scalability – the application should be scalable as regards future development, capable of handling large amounts of contacts and able to handle a large changing number of users.

Since the application is programmed in pure Java, there is great scope as regards various hardware platforms, operating systems and computer architectures in which the application will run. The application is capable of running on a PC connected to the Internet via a Local Area Network (LAN) or a standalone PC connected to the Internet via a modem. The software required to run the application is a Java Runtime Environment to interpret the java program along with the Simplewire SDK.

2.2 SMS Application Overview

Simplewire is one of a number of bulk SMS providers/resellers. Simplewire provides several API's for different programming languages in order to send text messages. The choice for this project was the Java development kit. This provides the interface with Simplewires' gateway in the form of a Jar8 file (swsms.jar) that consists of three classes:

- *SMS Class* – the SMS object is used for setting all the properties needed to send a text message.
- *SMSCarrier Class* – contains data relating to the service providers that Simplewire supports.
- *SMSCarrierList Class* – is used internally by the SMS class.

---

8 A method of grouping several class files

Simplewire provides documentation, explaining these classes and their methods along with examples. In order to download the SDK, one must first register a Developer Account with Simplewire[9]. You are then given:

- *A Subscriber ID* – identifies the subscriber of a developer account.
- *Subscriber Password* – password needed to send messages through ones developer account.
- *Access to a Virtual Mobile Phone* – an online phone simulator, which can receive text messages (free of charge). It is accessed from within an individuals developer account (see Figure 7) [Simplewire].
- *A Virtual Mobile Phone Number* – address of the subscribers Virtual Mobile Phone.

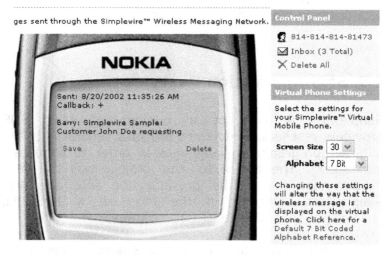

Figure 7: Simplewire's Virtual Phone [Simplewire]

One can then proceed to download Simplewires' Java SDK, which is packaged with the swsms.jar file, documentation and sample programs. Figure 8 shows such a program, which sends a text message to the authors Virtual Mobile Number.

---

[9] http://www.simplewire.com

```
/*********************************************************/
* Shows how to send a wireless message containing text in Java.*
*
* @author Simplewire, Inc. * @version 2.4.1 * @since  jdk1.2
/*********************************************************/

import com.simplewire.sms.*;

public class send_text
{
        public static void main(String[] args) throws Exception
        {
                SMS sms = new SMS();
                // Subscriber Settings
                sms.setSubscriberID("123-123-123-12345");
//Your Developer ID
                sms.setSubscriberPassword("12345678");
//Your Developer Password
                // Message Settings
                sms.setMsgPin("+1 100 511 6148");
//Destination Address
                sms.setMsgFrom("Demo");//Who Sent The Message
                sms.setMsgCallback("+1 100 555 1212");
//Senders Address
                sms.setMsgText("Hello World From Simplewire");
//The Actual Message
                System.out.println("Sending msg to Simplewire...");
                // Send Message
                sms.msgSend();
                // Check For Errors
                if(sms.isSuccess())
                {
                        System.out.println("Message was sent!");
                }
                else
                {
        System.out.println("Message was not sent!");
        System.out.println("Error Code: " + sms.getErrorCode());
        System.out.println("Error Descript: " + sms.getErrorDesc());
        System.out.println("Error res: "+sms.getErrorResolution()");
                }
        }
}
```

Figure 8: Simplewire Code to send message

Simplewire recommends that you develop your application in order to send text messages to your Virtual Mobile Phone first, and then you can buy message credits from Simplewire in order to send text messages to any mobile device.

One can first buy 500 demo message credits from Simplewire costing approximately $30 US dollars, which will allow you to send text messages to any mobile device but the message will include a "Simplewire Evaluation" tag at the beginning of each message. In order to eliminate the "Simplewire Evaluation" tag and gain access to the full spectrum of features offered by Simplewire, one must upgrade to a commercial account. All remaining demo message credits will be automatically transferred to ones commercial account [Simplewire].

The cost of a message depends on the network to which the message is being sent. One network may charge one credit per message and another could charge two credits per message. All network providers within the UK and Ireland charge 2 credits per text message. See Appendix H for a complete list of worldwide network providers supported by Simplewire and the amount of credits charged per message by each. See Table 2 below for credit purchase options offered by Simplewire [Simplewire].

Credits	$ US Dollars	Cents Per Credit	Cents Per Message in UK
1,000	57	5.7	11.4
10,000	450	4.5	9.0
50,000	1,900	3.8	7.6
100,000	3,600	3.6	7.2
250,000	8,250	3.3	6.6
500,000	14,500	2.9	5.8
1,000,000	20,000	2.0	4.0

Table 2: Simplewire Message Credits [Simplewire].

The application can now be designed since Simplewire has alleviated the problems associated with routing the text messages to the various service providers and provided a basic example of sending a text message. Figure 9 illustrates how this project implements Simplewires Wireless Messaging Protocol (WMP) into the process of sending a text message.

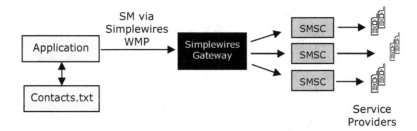

Figure 9: Sending a Short Message Using WMP

An overview of the system identifying the options and main process functions users navigate is presented in Figure 10.

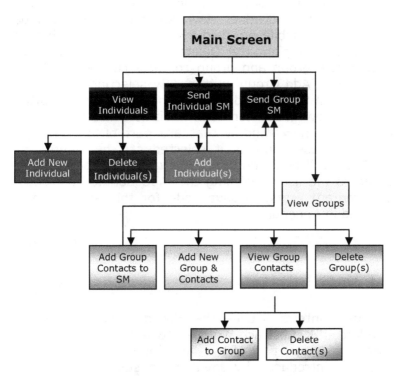

Figure 10: Design Overview.

Contacts are divided and stored into two sections, one for 'Individuals' the other for 'Groups' of individuals. A user will initially enter the main screen where they view

'Individuals' and have access to an input form to send a text message. From here the user can send a text message by typing directly in the Mobile no. field or by selecting one or several contacts from the list of individuals. Once a contact or contacts is selected from the list it can be added to the Mobile no. field by clicking the 'Add' button or deleted by clicking the 'Delete' button. A new individual can be added by clicking the 'Add Contact' button; this is also accessible on the main screen. From the main screen the user can switch from viewing 'Individuals' to viewing 'Groups' by clicking on the 'Groups' tab. In either view, a group text message can be sent by typing directly into the Mobile no. field the MSs destination address followed by a comma. The comma acts as a delimiter for a new mobile address. In the same way as in the individual view, selected groups can be added to the Mobile no. field by clicking the 'Add' button or deleted by clicking the 'Delete' button. In the 'Groups' view a new group and group contacts can be added by clicking the 'Add Group' button. By selecting one of the groups from the list and clicking on the 'Show All' button one can view group contacts. This is a list of contacts shown in a new window that are part of the selected group. These contacts if selected can be deleted by clicking the 'Delete' button. New group contacts can be added to the list by clicking the 'Add Contact' button. A full program listing in Java code for this application is included in Appendix J.

2.3 User Interface

The user interface uses the Swing package and the standard JDK Abstract Window Toolkit (AWT) package. Swing is a major part of the Java Foundation Class (JFC) that was introduced by JavaSoft to supersede AWT. A simple form is developed in the 'Interface' class that initially appears in a JFrame (a window) and later in a JPanel (section within a window) (see Figure 11). The program is capable of sending text messages through an interface. Although not seen in Figure 11 an extra JTextArea called 'feedback' is included in the interface. It has no border so it cannot be seen under normal conditions. As the name suggests it is used to inform the user of the status of message sending. For example, the code below is taken from the Interface class and displays the message "Message was sent" when the text message was sent successfully.

```
// Check For Errors
if(sms.isSuccess())
{
        System.out.println("Message was sent to " + aNumber + "!");
        feedback.setText("Message was sent");
}
```

The inclusion of the StringTokenizer class enables several numbers to be read in as tokens and subsequently sent as a group text message. But this requires the user to type the numbers into the Mobile No. field. A main screen is used to hold all the separate components of the application.

Figure 11: The User Input Form.

The main screen is developed through the FinalTest class. Several illustrations were made of the proposed main screen as illustrated in Figure 12.

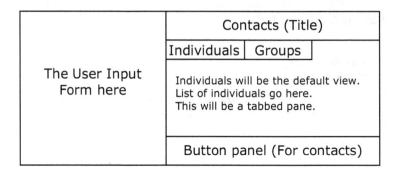

The User Input Form here	Contacts (Title)	
	Individuals	Groups
	Individuals will be the default view. List of individuals go here. This will be a tabbed pane.	
	Button panel (For contacts)	

Figure 12: The Proposed Main Screen.

From the illustration in Figure 12 we can see that the main screen is divided into two. With the user input form on the left and contact details on the right, which can switch from 'Individuals' to 'Groups' using the tabs.

A list of contacts (stored locally as a .txt file) is displayed under the 'Individuals' tab in the main screen. Firstly contacts must be added to a .txt file. This is achieved by creating an 'Add Contact' button and placing it in the button panel (under the tabbed pane).

```
addContactButton = new JButton("Add Contact");
addContactButton.addActionListener(new ActionListener() {

        public void actionPerformed(ActionEvent actionevent)
    {
                String name = "contacts";
                AddContact addcontact = new AddContact(name);

    addcontact.setDefaultCloseOperation(JFrame.HIDE_ON_CLOSE );
    setVisible( false );

    }

});
```

When clicked it calls on the AddContact class. Since AddContact extends JFrame the main screen is made invisible and the AddContact window appears (see Figure 13). The Add Contact window displays a simple form, which is displayed by calling the TextForm class. This form allows you to enter first name, last name, mobile number and email address. When the user clicks on the 'Add Contact' button the data entered into the form is sent to the contacts.txt file or creates a contacts.txt file if it does not exist.

Figure 13: The Add Contact Window.

Contacts are entered into the contacts.txt file as follows:

Lastname|Firstname|Mobile number|Email address

For example:

Balboa|Rocky|+35387986859|rocky@hotmail.com

'|' acts as a delimiter for each field. When the mobile number is entered a '+' sign is automatically added. Contacts are added to the contacts.txt file as a new line.

Contacts can be viewed in the 'Individuals' tabbed pane, which is the default pane. This is achieved by setting up a DisplayContacts class that extends JPanel and add it to the main screen (FinalTest class). The DisplayContacts class takes the name of the .txt file it has to display as an argument. The DisplayContacts class uses three other classes in the following order:

- *Contact class* – reads in contacts from the .txt file the DisplayContacts class has to display, in this case contacts.txt file and takes first name, last name, mobile number and email address as parameters.
- *Sorts class* – used to sort an array of Contacts into alphabetic order.
- *DisplayTextForm class* – used to format the sorted Contacts so that they are displayed starting with a checkbox, followed by name, mobile number and finally email address.

Since screen size is limited the DisplayContacts class places the formatted contact list into a JScrollPane so that the user can scroll down the list of contacts. Users can add contacts and view them through the 'Individuals' pane but the contacts does not interact with the input form. In order for this to happen an "Add" button is placed in the button panel so that when the user selects contacts by clicking on their checkbox, their mobile number can be added to the 'Mobile No.' field by clicking the 'Add' button. This is achieved by the following code.

```
addButton = new JButton("<< Add");
addButton.addActionListener(new ActionListener() {

public void actionPerformed(ActionEvent actionevent)
  {
  String numbers = "";
    numbers += messagePanel.numberfield.getText();
    for(int i=0; i<contacts.contacts.length; i++) {
        if(contacts.form.checkBox[i].isSelected()) {
        numbers += contacts.contacts[i].getMobileNumComma();
                    }//end if
    } //end for
  messagePanel.numberfield.setText(numbers);
        }
});
```

For speed and simplicity a 'Check All' checkbox is included in the button panel so that all 'Individuals' can be selected and deselected simultaneously with a single click. This is achieved as follows:

```
checkAll = new JCheckBox ("Check All");
checkAll.addActionListener(new ActionListener() {

public void actionPerformed(ActionEvent actionevent)
   {
          for(int i=0; i<contacts.contacts.length; i++) {
          if(checkAll.isSelected())
          contacts.form.checkBox[i].setSelected(true);
       else
          contacts.form.checkBox[i].setSelected(false);
   }
 }
});
```

Lastly to enable users to delete contacts a 'Delete' button was added to the button panel, which deleted only selected contacts. This involved overwriting the contacts.txt file with those contacts that were not selected. The code is as follows:

```
deleteButton = new JButton("Delete");
deleteButton.addActionListener(new ActionListener() {

public void actionPerformed(ActionEvent actionevent)
   {
          try {
          FileWriter writer = new FileWriter( "contacts.txt", false);
          PrintWriter pw = new PrintWriter( writer, true);
          for(int i=0; i<contacts.contacts.length; i++) {
          if(contacts.form.checkBox[i].isSelected()==false) {
          pw.println( contacts.contacts[i].getLastName() + "|" +
          contacts.contacts[i].getFirstName() + "|"
          contacts.contacts[i].getMobileNumPlain() + "|" +
          contacts.contacts[i].getEmail());
          }//end if
      } //end for
      pw.flush();
      pw.close();
      } catch (IOException exception) {
          System.out.println("Error adding contact");
          exception.printStackTrace();
          } //end catch
      setVisible( false );
      FinalTest finaltest = new FinalTest();
```

```
        finaltest.setDefaultCloseOperation(JFrame.EXIT_ON_CLOSE );
        }
});
```

When this is complete the default main screen will look like Figure 14.

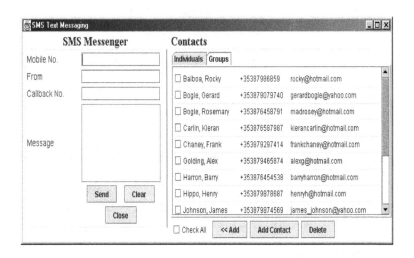

Figure 14: Main Screen in 'Contacts' View.

2.4 SMS Group Functionality

A list of groups, which are stored locally as .txt files are displayed under the 'Groups' tab in the main screen. Groups must be added to the groups.txt file and group contacts added to relevant groupname.txt files. This is achieved by creating an 'Add Group' button and placing it in the button panel in the main screen.

```
addGroupContactButton = new JButton("Add Group");
addGroupContactButton.setVisible(false);
addGroupContactButton.addActionListener(new ActionListener() {

public void actionPerformed(ActionEvent actionevent)
    {
        AddGroup addgroup = new AddGroup();
```

44

```
      addgroup.setDefaultCloseOperation(JFrame.HIDE_ON_CLOSE );
   setVisible( false );
 }
});
```

As we can see from the code above the button is initially made invisible, this is because the groups view is not the default contacts view and is only made visible when the user clicks on the 'Groups' tab. This is the same for all buttons used within the groups view. When the user clicks on the 'Add Group' button the AddGroup class appears as a new window and the main screen is made invisible (see Figure 15). The Add Group window is very similar to the Add Contact window as it also displays a form, which is displayed by calling the TextForm class. In addition to first name, last name, mobile number and email address this form enables you to enter a group name. When the user clicks on the 'Add Contact' button the data entered into the form is divided into two:

The group name is added to the groups.txt file as a new line or creates a groups.txt file if it does not exist. The last name, first name, mobile number and email address is added in that order to a .txt file with its name as the data entered into the group name field. For example in Figure 15 this file would be Classmates.txt. This is known as the group contacts file.

Figure 15: The Add Group Window.

Group contacts are entered into the groupname.txt file in the same format as individual contacts are entered into the contacts.txt file with '|' acting as a delimiter.

Now that a groups.txt file exists and groups have been entered along with their associated groupname.txt file, the groups must be viewed in the 'Groups' tabbed pane. This is achieved by setting up a DisplayTheGroups class that extends JPanel and add it to the main screen (FinalTest class). The DisplayTheGroups class will require three other classes in the following order:

- *Group class* – reads in groups from groups.txt file and takes group name as a parameter.
- *Sorts class* – used to sort an array of Groups into alphabetic order.
- *DisplayGroups class* – used to format the sorted Groups so that they are displayed starting with a checkbox, followed by group name.

DisplayTheGroups class also places the formatted group list into a JScrollPane so that the user can scroll down the list of groups if needed. In order for the 'Groups' pane to interact with the input form anther "Add" button must be placed in the button panel on the main screen so that when the user selects groups by clicking on their checkbox, their group contacts mobile number can be added to the 'Mobile No.' field by clicking the 'Add' button. This is achieved by the following code.

```
addButtonGroup = new JButton("<< Add");
addButtonGroup.setVisible(false);
addButtonGroup.addActionListener(new ActionListener() {

public void actionPerformed(ActionEvent actionevent)
    {
            String numbers = "";
            numbers += messagePanel.numberfield.getText();
            for(int i=0; i<groups.groups.length; i++) {
            if(groups.form.checkBox[i].isSelected()) {
    contacts2 = new GatherGroupContacts(groups.groups[i].getName());
            System.out.println(groups.groups[i].getName());

      for(int x=0; x<contacts2.contacts.length; x++) {
          System.out.println(contacts2.contacts[x].toString());
          numbers += contacts2.contacts[x].getMobileNumComma();
      } // end inner for
```

```
                            }//end if
      } //end outer for

    messagePanel.numberfield.setText(numbers);
  }

});
```

Two 'Add' buttons exist in the button panel but only one can be seen at any one time. When the user switches between the 'Individuals' and 'Groups' view, buttons are made visible or invisible depending on which view the user is on. From the code above we can see that another class GatherGroupContacts is used to read in the groups that are selected and output to string the list of mobile numbers that correspond to these groups. The GatherGroupContacts class will require two classes in the following order:

- *Contact class* – reads in group contacts from groupname.txt file and takes first name, last name, mobile number and email address as parameters.
- *Sorts class* – used to sort an array of Contacts into alphabetic order.

As in the 'Individuals' view a 'Check All' checkbox is included in the button panel so that all 'Groups' can be selected and deselected simultaneously with a single click. A 'Delete' button was also added to the button panel, which deletes only selected groups. This involved overwriting the groups.txt file with those groups that were not selected and deleting the relevant groupname.txt files. The code is as follows:

```
deleteButtonGroup = new JButton("Delete");
deleteButtonGroup.setVisible(false);
deleteButtonGroup.addActionListener(new ActionListener() {

public void actionPerformed(ActionEvent actionevent)
  {
        try {
        FileWriter writer = new FileWriter( "groups.txt", false);
        PrintWriter pw = new PrintWriter( writer, true);
```

```
for(int i=0; i<groups.groups.length; i++) {
    if(groups.form.checkBox[i].isSelected()) {
    String groupfilename = groups.groups[i].getName() + ".txt";
    // Ref: modified code accessed from:
    // http://javaalmanac.com/egs/java.io/pkg.html
    boolean success = (new File(groupfilename)).delete();
    if (!success)
            System.out.println("Failed to delete group file");
    }//end outer if
    else if(groups.form.checkBox[i].isSelected()==false) {
            pw.println( groups.groups[i].getName() );
    }//end else if
} //end for
pw.flush();
pw.close();
} catch (IOException exception) {
    System.out.println("Error adding contact");
    exception.printStackTrace();
    } //end catch
    setVisible( false );
    FinalTest finaltest = new FinalTest();
    finaltest.setDefaultCloseOperation(JFrame.EXIT_ON_CLOSE );
    }
});
```

Groups and individuals can be viewed in the main screen and a 'Show All' button in the button panel on the main screen shows all contacts in each group. When the user clicks on the 'Show All' button the ShowGroupContacts class appears as a new window on top of the main screen (see Figure 16). This window known as the group details window displays the group contacts for the selected group. The group details window can only display details for one group at a time otherwise an error message is displayed. The group details window like the main screen displays the group contacts in the same way as the contacts are displayed in the 'Individuals' tabbed pane by using the DisplayContacts class. The selected group name and ".txt" is passed to the DisplayContacts class as an argument.

The group details window allows you to add contacts to the group being viewed by clicking on the 'Add Contact' button. This displays the add contact window explained earlier in 'Contacts' – 'Individuals' view, but instead of the data entered into the form being sent to the contacts.txt file, the data is sent to the groupname.txt file which is being viewed. In this case when the add contact window appears and the group details window disappears.

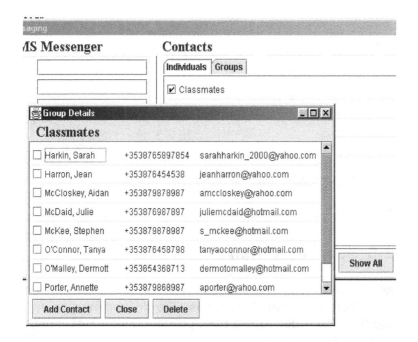

Figure 16: The Group Details Window.

Two other buttons are accessible on the group details window:

- 'Delete' button to delete selected group contacts.
- 'Close' button to close the group details window.

When this is complete the main screen in 'Contacts' – 'Groups' View will look like Figure 17.

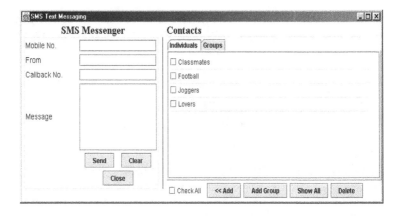

Figure 17: Main Screen in 'Contacts' View.

2.5 Security Details

At present the application is contained within the FinalTest class, which extends JFrame and has no main method. In order to run the application FinalTest must be called within a class which contains a main method. The Implementation class is used to call the FinalTest class within its main method. At this stage the application is complete and running but has no control over who uses it. As identified earlier in order to send a text message via Simplewires WMP the application must include Simplewires SDK and a valid subscriber Id and password set which is obtained by registering with Simplewire (www.simplewire.com). Thus in order to use the application an initial subscriber Id and password must be set. This is achieved through the Implementation class below.

```
//the entire application
import java.awt.*;
import java.awt.event.*;
import javax.swing.*;
import java.io.*;

public class Implementation
{
```

50

```
// execute application
public static void main( String args[] )
{
        File subscriberFile = new File( "subscriber.ini" );
        if ( subscriberFile.exists() )
        {
        FinalTest finaltest = new FinalTest();
        finaltest.setDefaultCloseOperation(JFrame.EXIT_ON_CLOSE );
        }
        else {
                Id_Password idpass = new Id_Password();
        idpass.setDefaultCloseOperation(JFrame.EXIT_ON_CLOSE );
                }
        }
}
```

The Implementation class checks if a subscriber.ini file exists locally in memory. If it does it calls the FinalTest class which displays the main screen. If the subscriber.ini file does not exist it calls the Id_Password class, which is displayed in a window as it extends JFrame (see Figure 18).

Figure 18: The Subscriber Id & Password Window

The subscriber Id and password window displays a simple form using the TextForm class. This form creates and stores the applications subscriber Id and password in a subscriber.ini file, which is later retrieved in the Interface class. This application can only be used by entering the authors' subscriber Id and password. This is controlled within the 'Ok' button as shown in code in Appendix H.

If the user enters the wrong subscriber Id or password an error message is displayed and the user is asked to try again. The subscriber Id and password window will only appear if a subscriber.ini file is not present. So that once the correct subscriber Id and password is set the subscriber Id and password window will not appear again and the Implementation class will display the main screen thereafter. When distributing the application the user of the system must know the subscriber Id and password. Otherwise the application will not run after setup. Also each application can be distributed with a different subscriber Id and password. For example, different organisations or users of this application will receive an application with their own subscriber Id and password so that only they could use it. This will allow easy management of applications, with each owner holding a different subscriber Id and password.

2.6 SMS Java Application User Guide

The application can be download freely from http://www.infm.ulst.ac.uk/~kevin/smsjava.zip. The Java application can be installed on several PCs on Windows, linux, solaris or macintosh platforms.

After installing the system the user clicks on the SMS Messenger application icon under the Start, Programs menu. The next screen will be a prompt to input a subscriber Id and password as shown in Figure 19. If an invalid subscriber Id and password is entered, then an error message is displayed as follows.

Invalid Subscriber Id and Password, please try again.

OK

Figure 19: Entering invalid Id & Password.

If a valid subscriber Id and password is entered, then the following message is displayed.

Subscriber Id & Password has been set successfully! Enjoy using the SMS Messenger Application.

OK

Figure 20: Entering a valid Id & Password.

When the 'Ok' button is clicked on the previous dialog window the main screen is shown as in Figure 21. As you can see the application contains no contacts, as the user must input them.

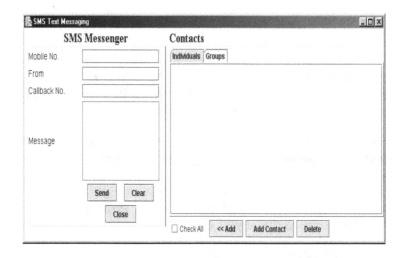

Figure 21: Application Main Screen

2.6.1 Adding Contacts to the System

From the main screen shown above the user clicks on the 'Add Contact' button. This opens up the add contact window. Several different contacts can be added. All fields are required so if a field is left blank, then the following warning message appears.

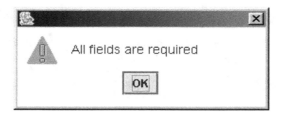

Figure 22: User Leaves a Required Field Blank.

The add contact form is validated in various ways. For instance if the user enters non-numeric data into the 'Mobile No.' field, then a warning message is displayed (see Figure 23).

54

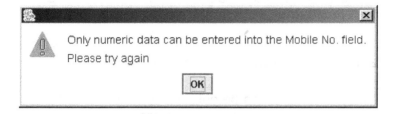

Figure 23: Non-numeric Data in 'Mobile No.' Field

If the user enters an invalid email address a warning message is displayed (see Figure 24).

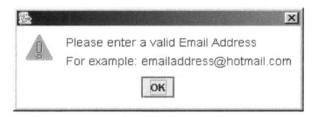

Figure 24: User Enters an Invalid Email Address.

If the user attempts to enter a contact whose first name and last name has been entered before an option message is displayed (see Figure 25). Users may wish to add the same contact name, for example in the case where the contact has two mobile phones, one for work, and the other for personal use.

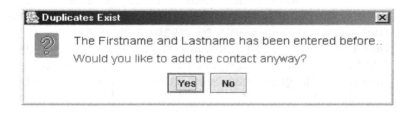

Figure 25: Firstname & Lastname repeated

Contacts are sorted in alphabetic order by last name and then first name.

2.6.2 Adding Contacts to the System

The groups view can be entered by clicking on the Groups tab as shown in Figure 26. The user knows that they are in the groups view because the 'Groups' tab turns blue and the button menu changes.

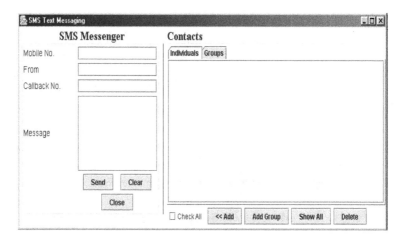

Figure 26: Main Screen – 'Groups' View

In order to add groups the user clicks on the 'Add Group' button. This opens the add group window as shown in Figure 26. The user can create a group by only filling in the 'Group Name' field or create a group and add a group contact by filling in all fields. If all fields are empty except the 'Group Name' field, the application assumes that the user only wants to create a new group. If no fields are empty the application assumes that the user wants to create a group and add a group contact to that group. If the group has been entered before, the contact is added to that group. When the user clicks on the 'Add Contact' button, the group and group contact is added and all fields are reset except for the 'Group Name' field, which displays the last group name entered. This allows

56

the user to enter contacts to that group without having to retype the group name in again. If the user wishes to add group contacts all fields must be filled in. The form is validated in the same way as the add contact form is validated. When sufficient groups and group contacts have been entered and the add group window is closed the main screen in 'Groups' view will appear. Groups are sorted in alphabetic order. In order to view group contacts the user must select a group from the list by clicking on its corresponding checkbox and then click the 'Show All' button. This displays the group details window. If no group is selected the following warning message is displayed.

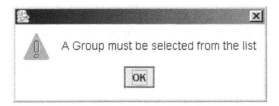

Figure 27: The User Has Selected no Group.

Only one group can be shown at the one time, so if more than one group is selected when the user clicks the 'Show All' button the warning message in Figure 28 is displayed.

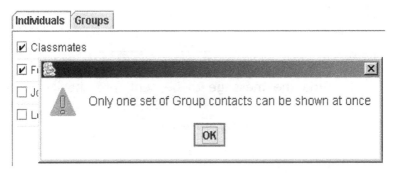

Figure 28: View one group only at a Time

The group details window displays contacts in alphabetic order by last name and then first name as in the

'Individuals' view on the main screen. From this screen the user can also add contacts to the group by clicking the 'Add Contact' button. This displays the add contact window. The user can add contacts to the group details window in the same way as adding contacts to the 'Individuals' view in the main screen.

2.6.3 Sending an Individual Text Message

A user can send an individual text message from the main screen regardless of what view they are in by carrying out the following:

1. Type the mobile number directly into the 'Mobile No.' field. Including a '+' sign at the start followed by the country code i.e. +353 and lastly the mobile devices address.

   ```
   +353876171700
   ```

2. Type who the message is from into the 'From' field.

   ```
   Barry
   ```

3. Type the address of the sender into the 'Callback No.' field.

   ```
   +353876454538
   ```

4. Type the message to be sent into the 'Message' field.

   ```
   How are you today
   ```

5. When 1-4 is complete click on the 'Send' button.

A successful send will be indicated to the user by the message "Message was sent" appearing in the feedback JTextArea explained earlier and shown in Figure 29.

Figure 29: Successful Send Message

The recipient will then receive the message on their mobile device as shown in Figure 30. The 'Simplewire Evaluation' tag is present and remains until the developers account is upgraded to a commercial account.

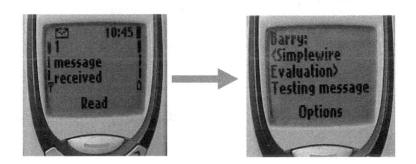

Figure 30: Message Delivered to Mobile Device.

The 'Mobile No.' field is the only field required to send a message. If it is blank when the user clicks the 'Send' button the following message will appear in the feedback text area.

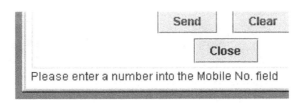

59

Figure 31: 'Mobile No.' field left blank

Otherwise if any of the other fields are left blank when the user clicks 'Send', the message is sent but these details are left out of the text message. Thus it is possible to send a text message without stating who sent it. Since the application requires an Internet connection the user receives an error message if a connection does not exist (see Figure 32). Also notice the message in the feedback text area in the bottom left hand corner of the screen.

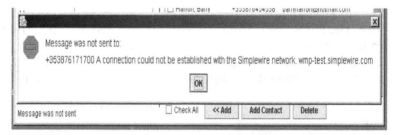

Figure 32: Application cannot find a connection.

All error message descriptions resulting from a send are taken from the Simplewire Wireless Messaging Platform. For a list of these errors and their descriptions see Appendix K. Three common errors resulting from a send are as follows:

- If the user enters non-numeric data into the 'Mobile No.' field (see Figure 33).
- If the user enters non-numeric data into the 'Callback No.' field (see Figure 34).
- If the user enters more characters than is allowed by the recipients' service provider (see Figure 35).

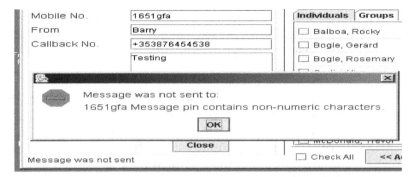

Figure 33: Non-numeric Data in Mobile No. field

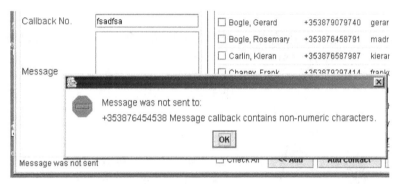

Figure 34: Non-numeric Data in Callback No. field

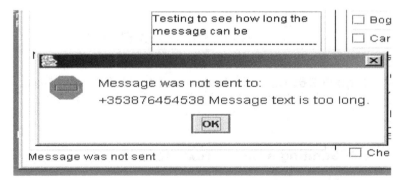

Figure 35: Service providers character limit exceeded

Another method of sending an individual text message is by inserting data into all text fields except the 'Mobile No.' field. and instead of typing directly into the 'Mobile No.' field. The user:

- Selects a contact from the 'Individuals' list by selecting its corresponding checkbox.
- Clicks the 'Add' button, which transfers the contacts mobile number to the 'Mobile No.' field followed by a comma, which acts as a delimiter for group sending.

The user can then click 'Send' to send the message. See diagram below.

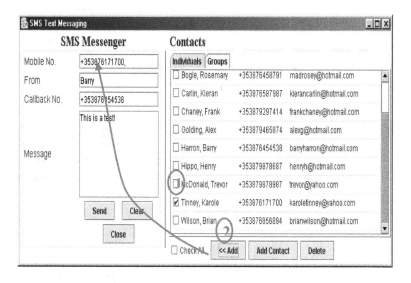

Figure 36: User adds contact to Mobile No. field

2.6.4 Sending a Group Text Message

Sending group text messages like individual text messages can be achieved by typing directly into the 'Mobile No.' field and/or by selecting contacts from the list. Using the direct method, the user types the mobile number into the 'Mobile No.' field followed by a comma and proceeds by typing another mobile number and so on. The user enters data into the remaining fields and clicks 'Send'. Using the selection method, the user may select several contacts from the 'Individuals' view and by clicking the 'Add' button will send their corresponding mobile numbers to the 'Mobile No.' field with commas added automatically. The user may then proceed to the 'Groups' view and select several groups from the list and by clicking the 'Add' button will send their corresponding group contact mobile numbers to the 'Mobile No.' field also with commas added automatically (see Figure 37).

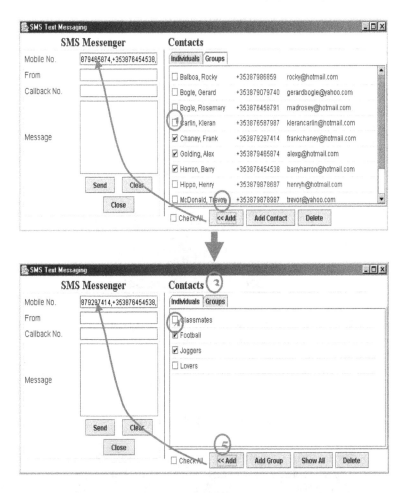

Figure 37: Adding mobile number to group

When the user moves between views using the tabs, selected groups or selected contacts become deselected so as to avoid confusion. This however forces the user to click 'Add' twice. The user can select all contacts from the 'Individuals' view quickly by selecting the 'Check All' checkbox in the button panel (see Figure 38). Likewise the user can select all groups from the 'Groups' view by selecting the 'Check All' checkbox. When the user has added the required mobile numbers the user enters data into the remaining fields and clicks 'Send'.

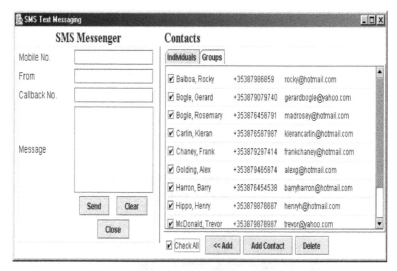

Figure 38: All Contacts Selected

The group send process performs error checking and validation in the same way as in sending an individual text message.

2.6.5 Deleting Contacts and Groups

In order to delete contacts from the 'Individuals' view the user must select contacts from the list and click the 'Delete' button on the button panel. This refreshes the screen showing clearly that the contacts are deleted (see Figure 39).

In order to delete groups and their contacts from the 'Groups' view the user must select groups from the list and click the 'Delete' button on the button panel. This refreshes the main screen, showing the 'Individuals' view. When the user returns to the groups view it will be clear that the groups are deleted.

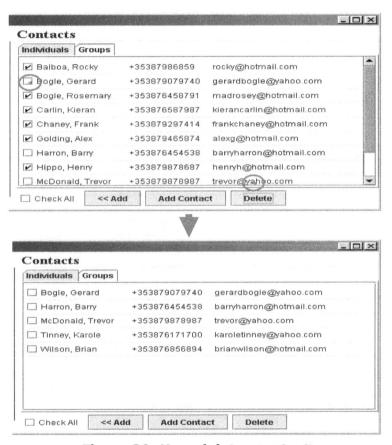

Figure 39: User deletes contacts

If the user wants to delete group contacts the user must enter the groups view and view group contacts. This displays the group details window. The user must then select group contacts from the list and click the 'Delete' button. This refreshes the group details window showing clearly that the group contacts are deleted (see Figure 40).

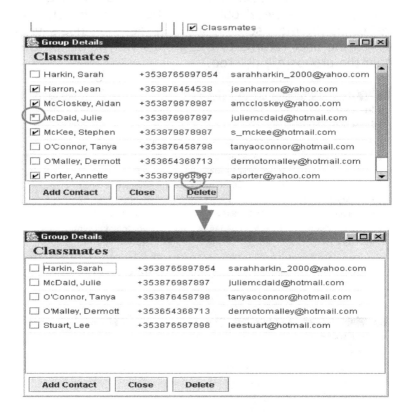

Figure 40: User deletes group contacts

2.6.6 Performance and Efficiency

Contacts are stored and retrieved from .txt files, which take up very little disk space. To store 1,000 contacts only takes up 52 kilobytes of disk space. The application itself takes up 26.2 megabytes of storage with only 3.77 megabytes needed to run the application itself, provided the terminal has a JRE already installed. Unfortunately the remaining 22.4 megabytes taken up by the JRE must be installed so as to guarantee that the application will run. In order to test the performance of sending text messages using the application, ten messages were sent from a standalone PC with Internet connection via a 56k modem. The table below shows the results.

2.6.7 Application Limitations

The SMS Messenger application implemented in this project is far from full proof. The application has several limitations outlined below:

- Input validation – mobile numbers have to include country codes and a '+' symbol, this could be alleviated by using a combo box or making a default country code. The email address is only validated by seeking a '@' symbol.
- User documentation and support – the application at present has no help procedure or any user manuals.
- Use of shortcut keys, for example 'Alt – s' to send a text message.
- The application can only display group details for one group at a time.
- The application launcher is not customised as it references InstallAnywhere during set up.
- Need to upgrade to a commercial account with Simplewire in order to drop the 'Simplewire Evaluation' tag.
- Consideration must be given to error handling.
- Cost of sending a text message within the UK up to 11.4 cents.
- User must ensure that the terminal is connected to the Internet.

2.6.8 Future Considerations

In order for the SMS Messenger application to be considered complete, certain additional functionality would be required.   Future work for perhaps, undergraduate students working on extending this application for a project may include:

- The ability to receive text messages and view them from an 'Inbox'.

- Allow the user to set the callback number in advance.

- Allow the user to save drafts and messages sent.

- Allow the user to send a text message and/or an email to a contact or group of contacts.

- Ability to receive email & view them from an 'Inbox'.

- Pre-program messages into memory and put into categories. For example a greetings category may contain a text message 'how are you today'.

- Develop EMS and MMS into the application. Simplewire already support ring tones, logos and picture messages.

- Incorporating instant messaging into the application.

- Eventually developing the application into a UMS.

3 An SMS ASP Application

This chapter presents an online SMS Active Server Page (ASP) application which can deliver a single text message to multiple employees simultaneously. The system can be placed online thus requiring no installation on the client-side, and incorporates a server-side contact database. This chapter describes the design and implementation of such a working prototype.

This application is presented in the form of an interface for the purpose of contacting IT support members of staff. By means of this system users are able to send individual and group SMS to relevant employees. The benefits of SMS in such an environment are excellent in comparison with traditional methods of communication such as the telephone or e-mail. SMS is much more cost effective than phone calls. Also individual means of contact are time consuming and laborious, with SMS groups can be contacted simultaneously. Since all members of support staff in the company are issued with a mobile phone, they may all be contacted instantly rather than waiting for them to check their e-mail. SMS also guarantees delivery of a message. Therefore any urgent messaging, such as a postponed meeting or changes to hardware will be relayed via this interface.

The scope of the prototype involves an online interface, with backend database connectivity. This database is built up around employee details, and accessed for the purpose of selecting individuals or groups to compose and send SMS messages to. For the purpose of sending SMS via the Internet, the Simplewire Active X Software Development Kit is used.

3.1 Dynamic Web Applications

As the Internet has developed, so too has its range of purpose and application. Web pages are no longer used solely for the purpose of providing information, as they were first designed to do. Today dynamic applications are the growing trend throughout the Web, involving user interactivity to search for information, complete forms, to request and to respond. The vast quantity of information, journals, and users means that for practicality's sake, many web sites must now incorporate connectivity to a server-side database, as Davidson comments: "By utilising database driven dynamic content delivery technology, Library web administrators can obtain numerous management benefits over a static HTML site" [Davidson01].

The main problem with using the web for dynamic data access lies with the fact that the language used, Hyper-Text Mark-up language (HTML), has little processing power past that of displaying static data [Yerkey01]. To allow dynamic user access to data and the ability to add existing data requires the use of other languages in addition to HTML. Since this project will be web-based and require connectivity to a Microsoft Access database, Web pages with dynamic attributes will be required. A number of different technologies exist to accomplish this, although each must be examined to find that which suits best.

3.1.1 Common Gateway Interface

The Common gateway Interface (CGI) was one of the first methods of server-side processing of user interaction. Programs written in the CGI standard take a user request from a Web page, access a database, and send the appropriate response to the user's browser, by creating lines of HTML code with embedded data. [Yerkey01]. Programs may be compiled in almost any language. The main problem with CGI however is that the compiled programs must reside on the server and for this reason is burdensome to administrators. CGI is also much slower to execute requests in comparison to the newer forms of server-side scripting, such as Active Server Pages (ASP). As the main functionality exits in a program, experienced programmers must create applications, making CGI a more complicated and more costly option.

3.1.2 Practical Extraction Report Language (PERL)

An open-source programming language, PERL was originally developed for UNIX, but now exists in versions for UNIX, Linux, DOS, and Windows 95/98/NT. It has a uniform syntax across all platforms, with a simple compile and execute structure [Copeland00]. PERL incorporates the same functions for both client and server-side scripting. Unfortunately, special installation is required on the client-side, making it less flexible [Copeland00]. Again, experienced programmers are required to create fully functional applications.

3.1.3 Java Server Pages (JSP)

Java Server Pages (JSP) are a relatively new dynamic Web page technology. Similar in many ways to Microsoft's Active Server Pages (ASP), they are aimed towards those who simply must build all applications using pure Java. While providing much of the same functionality of ASP, the pages are platform independent and allow developers to create their own custom tags. According to Sun, the technology's developer, the main advantage is that: "JSP technology uses the Java language for scripting, while ASP pages use Microsoft VBScript or JScript. The Java language is a mature, powerful, and scalable programming language that provides many benefits over the Basic-based scripting languages" [Sun02].

While JSP certainly have advantages, the fact remains that they are a fledgling technology, in many ways providing too complex a service for what is required in this project. If all that is required is a dynamic web site with database connectivity, then JSP could be a case of overkill, due to the multitude of skills, tools and techniques involved.

3.1.4 PHP

PHP (recursive acronym for "PHP: Hypertext Preprocessor") is an Open-Source scripting language that can be easily embedded into HTML. It is an effective scripting language for adding a dynamic content to Web pages that has proved effective by way of ease of learning and its extensibility. It has become popular on Microsoft platforms through the Foxserv bundle of Apache, using a combination of apache HTTP Server, PHP and a database system such as mySQL [Connolly02]. The downside of PHP however are found to be weak abstraction from server side databases and the fact that it is viewed by many programmers as lacking true language structure due to untyped variables.

3.1.5 Active Server Pages (ASP)

Active Server Pages (ASP) is a programming model allowing dynamic Web pages to be created and executed on the Web server. ASP files have the extension '.asp', and contain text, HTML tags and scripting [Connolly02]. The great advantage that ASP has is that it is the best suited option for deployment in a complete windows environment, having been developed by Microsoft, which is precisely what this project requires. The server involved must be running a Windows application, with Internet Information Server (IIS) installed. For development purposes on a Windows 95/98 or NT Workstation, though not for Web deployment, Microsoft Personal Web Server (PWS) is available, allowing the pages to be created and tested in a familiar and easily accessible environment. The technology has a number of advantages over other dynamic development strategies:

72

- Full use of a programming language is not required to create dynamic pages.
- It is significantly faster than CGI.
- ASP is multithreaded, able to handle large volumes of users
- The user requires nothing more than a browser to interact, the Web provides an interface.
- ASP imbeds the script within the Web page, meaning less overhead than stand alone programs, such as those for CGI that execute when called by the web page [Yerkey01].
- Scripts are run on the server rather than the client, so there are no concerns on whether or not a user's browser can handle the scripting.
- Only the script's results are viewable from the browser, processing logic is hidden [Copeland00].

Perhaps the greatest advantage of ASP is the ability to use and implement ready-made programmable components, Active X Data Objects (ADO). Yerkey describes these as:

"...pre-packaged programming libraries that are built into the Web server and called upon to do some work when it needs to be done. ADO relieves the programmer from writing code for every little thing that he/she wants to do." [Yerkey01]. Originally designed for database connectivity, version 2.5 has seen its capabilities extended to encompass a wide variety of programming uses. The components may also be composed in a wide variety of languages, such as C++, Visual Basic and Borland Delphi. ASP therefore is clearly the most suitable choice for incorporating Simplewire's C++ COM object, and the best to use in a Windows environment as specified by the user requirements.

3.1.6 Scripting

Scripting languages play an essential role in dynamic web applications due to their simplicity and portability. They allow the creation of functions embedded within HTML code, meaning objects can be accessed and manipulated, and various processes automated. (Connolly, 2002).

For Server-side scripting, ASP uses VBScript. VBScript is a Microsoft procedural language, with a similar syntax to Visual Basic. It may be executed within the browser or at the server before the document is sent [Connolly02]. VBScript is an efficient Server-side scripting language providing all the operations, such as that of database connectivity, which a dynamic application requires. The scripts are placed within **<%** and **%>** symbols.

Javascript is not a relational language to Java, but rather a separate object-based scripting language. It is a runtime language, as opposed to Java's compile-time system: "It is a very simple programming language that allows HTML pages to include functions and scripts that can recognise and respond to user events such as mouse clicks, user input, and page navigation." [Connolly02].

For the majority of Client-side scripting in this prototype, JavaScript is used, in particular for validation, although some Client-side VBScript will also be used. This is due to the fact of the non-recognition of VBScript by Netscape browsers. The code is placed within <SCRIPT LANGUAGE="JavaScript"> and </SCRIPT> tags.

3.1.7 Backend Databases

Connolly describes a Database Management System (DBMS) as "A software system that enables users to define, create, maintain, and control access to the database." [Connolly02]. There are advantages to placing such a system online:

- Platform Independence- traditional database clients require large modifications to function cross-platform, access through a browser eliminates this concern.

- Graphical User Interface- provides a simplistic and more navigable process of accessing the DBMS.
- Transparent Network Access- eliminates the need for costly networking software, and the difficulties in getting different platforms to talk to one another [Connolly02].

A back-end, server based DBMS therefore provides a complication-free means of information access, provided through that most familiar of interfaces, the web browser. Developed as part of Microsoft's Web Solution Platform, Open Database Connectivity (ODBC) is the company's popular Application Programming Interface (API) for database access. When used through ASP, database access is through use of the Structured Query Language (SQL) embedded in the VBScript code. The technology involved allows access to multiple DBMS from a single application. This is the connectivity that will be employed by us in this chapter.

Microsoft Personal Web Server can be used for testing purposes. This basically provides your PC with a web server. Microsoft Personal Web Server can be installed by first inserting a Windows 98 CD-ROM in the CD-ROM drive.

1. Click **Start**, and then click **Run**.
2. In the **Open** box, type the following path to the Setup.exe file, where *x* is the letter of your CD-ROM drive:
3. **x:\add-ons\pws\setup.exe**
4. Click **OK**.
5. Follow the instructions in Personal Web Server Setup.

The PWS can then be run by navigating to *Start/Programs/Accessories/InternetTools/Personal Web Manager* and clicking on the icon.

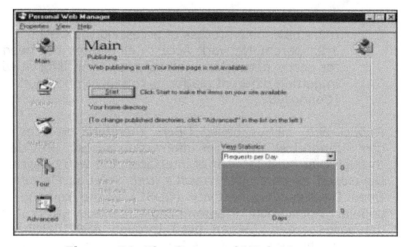

Figure 41: The Personal Web Manager

Once the Personal Web Manager is started, the IP address of the PC is displayed as is the directory into which files must be stored to make them online which is by default *C: //Inetpub/wwwroot.*

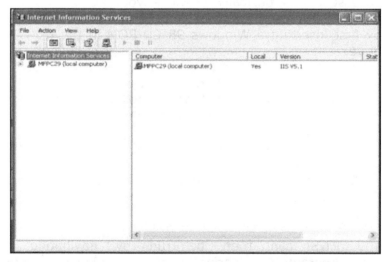

Figure 42: Internet Information Services

The application can also be hosted using Information Server (IIS), which is a feature of Windows 2000 and above (see Figure 42). It is activated by selecting:

Start/ControlPanel/Add/Remove Programs/Add/ Remove Windows Components.

The option to add IIS is then checked, and it is loaded from the Windows CD. The Service can be administrated by selecting Internet Information Services from Administrative Tools.

3.2 ASP Application Design

What follows is an overall process model of the SMS ASP prototype system.

Login – access to the interface is controlled by means of a registered login and password. If the correct fields are not entered the user must return to the login page and retry. Only when the proper login and password are entered can the user proceed to the homepage.

Home – upon arrival at the homepage the user is presented with three separate options, to add an employee, to search for an employee or employees, or to send a manual SMS.

Add Employee – the user may add an employee by completing the required fields, first and last name, mobile number, job title and region. Once submitted, the new details are added to the database and displayed to the user.

Manual SMS – here the user may compose and send an SMS message by entering a mobile number and message. Once submitted status of whether or not the message has been sent is displayed.

Search – to search the user can specify any combination of first name, last name, job title, and region or simply search to display all records of the database.

Results – from the results of the search the user may choose to edit details of a checked employee, delete any number of checked employees, or compose and send an SMS to any number of checked employees. The option also exists to compose and send an SMS to all. From the edit page, an employee's details may be updated or deleted.

The overall process flow is illustrated in Figure 43.

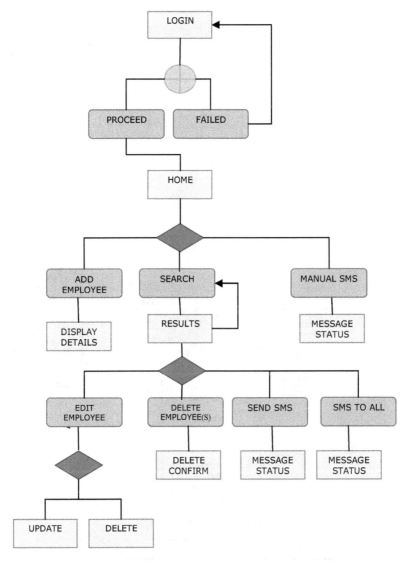

Figure 43: Overall Process Flow

Figure 44 outlines the internal and external links between ASPs throughout the interface, as well as the processes hidden from the user.

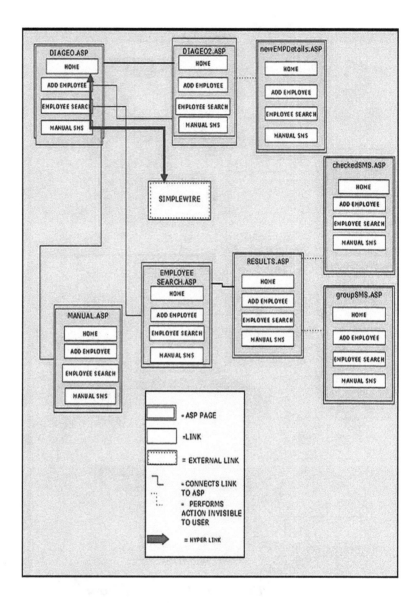

Figure 44: Web Map of the interface

Figure 45 displays the physical attributes to be employed by the system –

- Client
- Internet Information Service (IIS)
- Employee Database

80

- Simplewire Active X Component
- Short Message Service Center (SMSC)
- Network Transmitters
- Employee Mobile Telephones

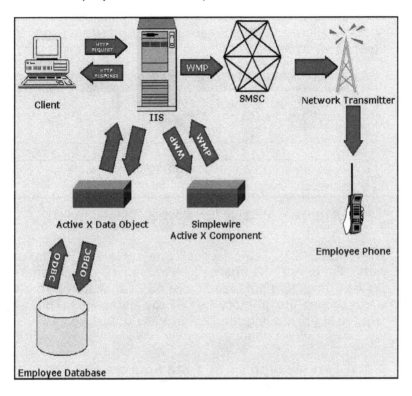

Figure 45: Physical Attributes of the system

3.3 Contacts Database Development

The software tools used in this section include Microsoft Access, Microsoft FrontPage for ASP design, and the Personal Web Server.

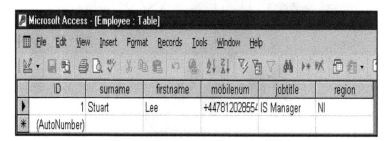

Figure 46: Table 'Employee' (Diageo.mdb)

The database is comprised of one table - 'Employee', with fields of 'Surname', 'Firstname', 'mobilenum', 'Jobtitle' and 'Region' (see Figure 46). An AutoNumber ID was used as the primary key of the database. This was created simply, using the Design View of Access.

3.3.1 Establishing ODBC Data Sources (32 Bit)

The next step is to assign it a Data Source Name (DSN). The DSN is the name that the database will be referred to in the ASP, and makes the connection between the name used in ASP and the actual database name [Yerkey01].

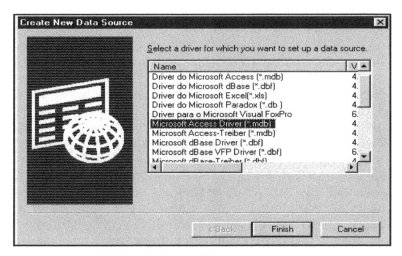

Figure 47: Specifying a Driver

The ODBC Data Sources (32 Bit) is located in the control panel of Windows. To make a connection three factors must be specified under the 'System DSN' tab:

1. The type of driver required - Microsoft Access Driver (*mdb) (see Figure 47).
2. The location of the database
3. The name by which it will be known- "Diageo" (see Figure 48).

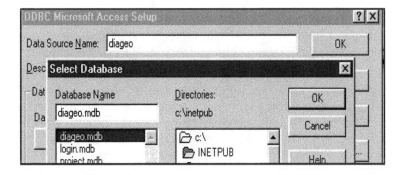

Figure 48: Selecting the database & applying DSN

3.4 Login Process

Users are unable to access any part of the interface unless a recognized login and password had been submitted. This would protect access to employee details, and also prevent the unsolicited sending of SMS messages. The first prototype presented to the user involved the hard coding of a login and password into the ASP scripting. It was decided however that this was not suitable for two reasons. This was firstly for security and secondly the fact that new users could not be added easily. Therefore it was decided that the login and password strings of verified users should be stored in a database, 'Login.mdb'. A simple table 'empLogin' was set up to hold login and password values.

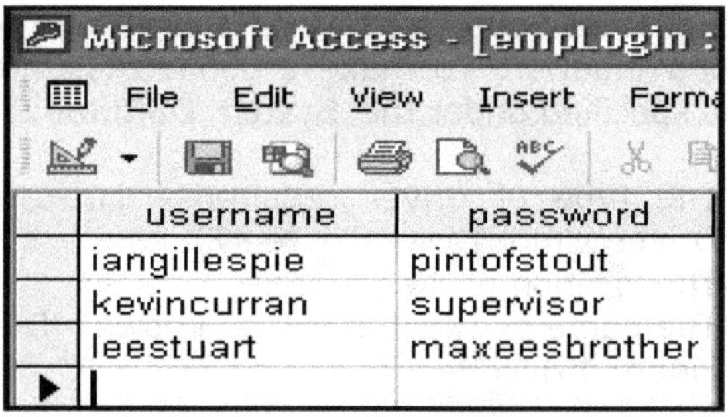

Microsoft Access - [empLogin :

File Edit View Insert Form

username	password
iangillespie	pintofstout
kevincurran	supervisor
leestuart	maxeesbrother

Figure 49: Table empLogin (Login.mdb)

The next step was to access this table from the 'Default.asp', and compare the values submitted by the user with those in fields 'username' and 'password'. Should the user input match these they may proceed to the homepage, otherwise they must make another attempt. The VBScript needed to achieve this incorporated a simple SQL request, comparing the user response from the page's form with the records of the database.

```
<%
else
 SQL = "SELECT * FROM empLogin " _
```

```
& "WHERE username='" & Replace(Request.Form("login"), "'", "''") & "' "
—
            &       "AND       password='"         &
replace(Request.Form("password"), "'", "''") & "';"
```

The connection to the database is then established:
```
Set Conn = Server.CreateObject("ADODB.Connection")
      Conn.Open("DRIVER={Microsoft Access Driver (*.mdb)};" _
      & "DBQ=" & Server.MapPath("login.mdb"))
      Set rs = Conn.Execute(SQL)
```

3.5 Adding an Employee

The addition of any information to a company database must be well regulated. The correct adding of an employee's details to the 'diageo.mdb' was therefore validated using client-side JavaScript. The form completed by the user could not be submitted if any of the fields were left blank.

```
<SCRIPT LANGUAGE="JavaScript">
<!--
function validateForm ( MyForm )
{
   if (MyForm.surname.value == ""){
     alert( "Please enter employee surname." );
   MyForm.surname.focus();
     return false ;
   }
```

In this instance the function checks if the 'surname' text box from the form is an empty string, if so an alert appears requesting the user to "Please enter employee surname'. When this alert is acknowledged the cursor focuses on the blank text box. The function is activated by placing it in the header of the HTML form.

```
<FORM NAME="MyForm"    onsubmit="return validateForm(this)   "
action="newEmpDet.asp">
```

It was also essential that the addition of mobile numbers to the database be carried out correctly. Again this was achieved with JavaScript.

```
var GoodChars = "0123456789+ "
for (var i =0; i <= MyForm.mobilenum.value.length -1; i++) {
```

```
if (GoodChars.indexOf(MyForm.mobilenum.value.charAt(i)) == -1) {
alert(MyForm.mobilenum.value.charAt(i) + " is an invalid character for a
mobile number.")
MyForm.mobilenum.focus();
```

Firstly the legal characters (0123456789+) are declared.
A 'for' loop then checks the entire length of the value
submitted by the user as an employee mobile number to
discover if anything other than these characters has been
entered. If so an alert appears informing the user of the
illegal character.

In order to add these details to the database, a server-
side VBScript had to be created that would firstly create a
connection object, and subsequently use this object to
add the form details to the appropriate field in the
'Employee' table.

```
<!-- #include file="adovbs.inc" -->
<%
Dim  Connect

Set Connect = Server.CreateObject("ADODB.RecordSet")
Connect.Open       "Employee",       "DSN=diageo",       adOpenKeyset,
adLockOptimistic
```

Firstly a recordset connection object 'Connect' is created, then used to
open access to the 'Employee' table.

```
Connect.AddNew
Connect.Fields("surname")= Request("surname")
Connect.Fields("firstname")= Request("firstname")
Connect.Fields("mobilenum")= Request("mobilenum")
Connect.Fields("jobtitle")= Request("jobtitle")
Connect.Fields("region")= Request("region")
Connect.Update
```

This object is then used to place the requested form data
in the appropriate database field. Subsequently the
details successfully added are displayed to the user using
HTML.

3.6 Searching for an Employee

The ability to successfully search the records of the database is a critical aspect in the functionality of the project. It is from the results of a search that the majority of SMS messages will be sent. The user must have the capability to search for an individual by completing one or more of the four search fields, as well as the ability to specify groups characterized by parameters such as job title or region. This was to be accomplished by the use of an SQL statement within the server-side VBScript.

Firstly the variables to be used are declared, and then assigned to the values of the form submitted for search by the user. The connection to the database is then opened.

```
<%
Dim Connect,jobtitleX, first, second, regionX
Dim Searcher, List

first = Request("firstnameX")
second = Request("surnameX")
jobtitleX = Request("jobtitleX")
regionX = Request("regionX")

Set Connect = Server.CreateObject("ADODB.Connection")
Connect.Open "diageo"
```

The next step is to create an SQL statement, named 'Searcher', which will select all the fields from a record that matches any of the values specified by the user's form submission. The variable 'Searcher' is first used to select all employee details:

```
Searcher   =   "SELECT   employee.*,   employee.surname,
employee.firstname,employee.mobilenum,   employee.jobtitle,
employee.region "
```

From the 'Employee' table

```
Searcher = Searcher & "FROM Employee"
```

With fields that have a sequence of characters of any length containing the form values submitted by the user.

```
Searcher = Searcher & "WHERE (((employee.surname) Like '%" &
second & "%')) AND (((employee.firstname) Like '%" & first & "%'))
AND (((employee.jobtitle) Like '%" & jobtitleX & "%')) AND
(((employee.region) Like '%" & regionX & "%'));"
```

If a match is not found then it is important that the user be made aware of this fact. The SQL is set to search from the beginning of the file until the end, if no records match, a message is displayed through HTML.

```
<% If rs.BOF and rs.EOF Then %>
<h2 align="center"><font face="Arial" size="3" color="#990033">No
match found</font></h2>
```

Matches that are found are displayed in HTML table format, with a checkbox also inserted for each record, so that individuals and groups may be selected for deletion, modification or to send an SMS.

3.7 Deleting Employees

The initial prototype received by the user gave the option to delete a single employee. Further specifications however requested the opportunity for a batch deletion. If for example the user searched for all employees in a region, and wished to delete all the results returned, then this must be accomplished.

Firstly it was important to make sure that an employee or employees had been selected for deletion. This involved client-side VBScript. A variable 'delete' is declared, and assigned the value of the ticked checked boxes requested from the form in 'Results.asp'. If this is an empty string then the user is requested to return to the previous page and select the appropriate employees.

```
<%
dim delete
delete=request("empID")
if delete="" then
response.write("<center><font face=Arial size=2 color=#990033>No
employee was selected to delete<P>")
```

```
response.write("<A Href=javascript:history.go(-1)> Go Back </A>")
```

Otherwise a connection is made to the database:

```
ELSE
Dim empID,   Conn, SQL
Set Conn = Server.CreateObject("ADODB.Connection")
Conn.Open "diageo"
```

This is assigned to an SQL statement that deletes those records in the database which correspond to the employees checked for deletion by the user:

```
SQL = "DELETE FROM employee " & _
            "WHERE ID IN (" & Delete & ")"
```

Finally confirmation is returned to the user of how many employees were successfully deleted:

```
Response.Write "<center><font face=Arial size=2 color=#990033>" &
Request("empID").Count & " employees were deleted...<BR>"
```

3.8 Editing an Employee

In any company there are constant shifts in employee details, as employees change role, region, or simply purchase a new mobile telephone. It was essential therefore to allow the user an easily accessible means to view employee details and update them. From the results of a search the user can select an employee to edit. Again VBScript validation was used to ensure that an employee had been selected, as well as a script to limit the editing to one employee at a time to prevent any errors occurring. If more than one employee had been selected for editing then the requested employee IDs would be returned as a string of digits separated by commas. Therefore a 'for' loop was composed that would check the length of this string for a comma:

```
 <%
dim strID
strID=request("empID")
```

```
Dim iStrPos, iLoop, strCurrentChar
For iLoop = 1 to Len(strID)
            strCurrentChar = Mid(strID, iLoop, 1)

    if strCurrentChar = "," _
```

If a comma was found, more than one employee had been selected for editing and a response was made to the user about this:

```
Then
response.write("<p      align=center><font      face=Arial      size=2
color=#990033>Please select only one employee to edit.</P>")
```

Otherwise the user is free to edit or delete the employee details that are displayed in HTML table form. The same JavaScript validation and database connection techniques that were employed in the adding of an employee are used.

3.9 Sending a SMS

The choice of the Simplewire Active X Software Development Kit meant that a ready message structure, address format, encoding and error structure were already in place and could be adhered to. The component can therefore be integrated into the VBScript of the ASP with appropriate parameters set, to enable SMS messages to be sent to individuals and groups.

3.9.1 Message Structure

The message structure consists of a request submission containing header, mandatory information and optional information which are sent to the SMSC using WMP, and a response submission with similar structure.

3.9.2 Request Submission

The request element determines what response will be gained from the SMSC. A WMP request header specifies the xml version, request version and request type.

```
<?xml version="1.0" ?>
<request version="2.0" protocol="paging" type="operation name">
</request>
```

The following table outlines the format of a message request. Its version (XML), protocol and type are contained in the header, whilst the mandatory parameters of subscriber ID, password and message PIN are set by the developer. The only optional parameter deemed necessary for this project is that of message text.

	Element	Attribute	Description
Header	Request	Version	Identifies the version of the request. Set to "2.0"
	Request	Protocol	Identifies the protocol contained within the request element. Set to "paging"
	Request	Type	Identifies the type of request, or the operation. Set to "sendpage"

Table 3: Format of a message request

Mandatory	Subscriber	Id	Identifies the ESME account requesting this operation.
	Subscriber	Password	The password used by the SMSC to authenticate the ESME request.
	Page	Pin	Identifies the destination address (e.g., the recipient) of the short message. Please refer to Section 4.1 - International Address Format for information about the proper format for this field.
Optional	Page	Text	Up to 140 octets (160 7-bit characters) of short message user data. This is typically 7-bit text, but may contain Unicode (16-bit) text as well. Proper HTML escaped entities may be used in place of characters. HTML entities are typically used to send 16-bit characters in a 7-bit data channel. Please refer to the *Option DataCoding* field for more information on sending anything other than 7-bit data.
	User	Agent	Contains information about the user agent originating the request. This is mostly for statistical purposes, but can be used for enforcing SMSC access to specific user agents. While this is an optional parameter, an ESME SHOULD include this field with requests. An example would be "ActiveX/SMS/2.4.2"

Table 4: Simplewire request message structure

3.9.3 Response Submission

Responses from the SMSC are contained in the body of the HTTP. The header of the message contains the response version, protocol and type. Included in the mandatory section is the success or failure response. Should a failure occur then the error code, description and resolution are displayed to the user in an HTML format.

	Element	Attribute	Description
Header	Response	Version	Identifies the version of the response. Will be set to "2.0"
	Response	Protocol	Identifies the protocol contained within the response element. Will be set to "paging"
	Response	Type	Identifies the type of response, or the operation response. Will be set to "checkstatus"
Mandatory	Error	Code	Indicates the success or failure of the submit request. The complete list of error codes is available at http://www.simplewire.com/developers/knowledge/reference/errors/
	Error	Description	A textual description of the numeric *Error Code* field which can be used to quickly debug its meaning.
	Error	Resolution	A textual description of ways that the Error Code can be overcome.
Optional	Ticket	Id	
	Ticket	Transmit	Number of SMS required to fully transmit entire submit request to MS. For example, some Smart Messages may need to be split up into 1-3 separate SMS "chunks" to be fully sent to the destination MS.
	Ticket	Price	Number of credits required to send each SMS.
	Ticket	Total	Total number of credits deducted from account balance.
	Ticket	Pin	Destination address of MS that will receive the message. Typically, this should be used to confirm the submit request was sent to the correct MS.

Table 5: Simplewire response message structure

3.9.4 Addressing Format

The Simplewire WMP employs an international addressing format for submissions to the SMSC, namely a format specifier, country code and national trunk. The '+'

character is used as the format specifier, followed by a numeric country code and trunk.

For example, a UK number would be set as '+44123456789', where '+' is the format, '44' the country code and '123456789' the following digits making up the destination address.

3.9.5 Encoding

Binary (8-bit) data sent over 7-bit communication channels requires the conversion of binary data into encoded characters. Each 8-bit octet is represented by two 7-bit encoded characters. (Simplewire, 2002). This reduction is necessary to allow the larger range of hexadecimal values possible with binary data to be successfully transmitted over a 7-bit medium.

3.9.6 Errors

The Active X component contains a built in error coding and description function, which ensures the user is constantly kept up to date with the status of the message. These are displayed in an HTML format when the message request has been received by the SMSC. Even a successfully sent message has its status returned in the form of an error code. Below are a few examples of the most common errors.

Error Code	Error Class	Error Description
0	Delivery	Message successfully sent to carrier.
1	Processing	Processing request.
2	Processing	Message successfully queued.
3	Delivery	Message buffered with carrier and waiting for delivery response.
4	Delivery	Message successfully delivered.
349	Syntax	Message pin contains non-numeric characters.
350	Syntax	A message pin is required.

Table 6: Message status, error code, class and description

3.10 Active X Component

The Active X SMS Component is utilized in three parts of the interface, sending a manual SMS, an individual or group SMS, or a SMS to everyone in the database.

3.10.1 Manual SMS

The manual SMS page is to be used by the user to send an SMS message to a mobile telephone regardless of whether or not the recipient is contained within the database. The user may simply enter a mobile number in international format, compose a message and send. The sending of a message is validated with client-side JavaScript to make sure that a valid mobile address has been entered, as in the addition of employee details. JavaScript is also used to ensure a text message has been composed before submission to the SMSC. The function checks to make sure that the text-area contained in the form is not an empty string.

```
if (frmSMS.msg.value=="") {
alert( "Please enter a text message." );
  frmSMS.msg.focus();
return false;
        }
```

The Active X component is called into use using VBScript and assigned to a variable 'sms':

```
Set sms = Server.CreateObject( "Simplewire.SMS" )
```

The subscriber settings of ID and password are then assigned to this variable, having been given when registering with Simplewire:

```
sms.SubscriberID = "382-022-271-04042"
sms.SubscriberPassword = "ED4D6318"
```

Next, the parameters are set. These are:
- Message Pin – the mobile number requested from the form the user has submitted
- Message From – who the message is from, set to the name of the user
- Callback – set as the Simplewire default
- Message Text – again requested from the form

```
sms.MsgPin =  Request.Form("nums")
sms.MsgFrom = "Ian Gillespie"
sms.MsgCallback = "+11005101234"
sms.MsgText = Left(Request.Form("msg"), 160)
```

The user is then presented with an acknowledgement that an attempt to send the message is underway:

```
Response.Write("<font   face=Arial   size=2   color=#990033>Sending
message...</font><br>")
```

The message is then sent:

```
sms.MsgSend
```

If the message is successfully sent the user is informed:

```
If (sms.Success) Then
Response.Write("<font face=Arial size=2 color=#990033>message was
sent!</font><br>")
```

Otherwise, the user is informed that the attempt was unsuccessful, and an error description is displayed:

```
Else
            Response.Write("<b>message was not
sent!</b><br>")
            Response.Write("Error Code: " & sms.ErrorCode &
"<br>")
            Response.Write("Error Description: " & sms.ErrorDesc
& "<br>")
            Response.Write("Error Resolution: " &
sms.ErrorResolution & "<br>")
```

3.10.2   Individual/Group SMS

When presented with the results of a search the user has the option to select which employees they wish to send a message to by ticking the checkbox beside the displayed names. The problem that was found to exist when developing the prototype was the fact that Simplewire do not support group messaging. At first this was seen as a major setback, but upon further research it was decided to attempt group messaging by creating a VBScript loop. This would prove to be a difficult task to overcome, but eventually success was achieved. Firstly the employee ID's checked from Results.asp are requested and assigned to a String.

```
String1=request("empID")
```

This string is then split into separate elements, using the comma between ID's as a delimiter. These elements are then assigned into an array 'aString':

```
aString=split(String1, ",")
```

A 'For' loop was then created to process each element in the array. A simple SQL statement selects from the database the mobile numbers of those employees whose ID matches that of an item in the array:

```
For each Item in aString
SQL="Select mobilenum FROM employee Where ID = " & Item
Set X = rs.Execute(SQL)
```

This statement is assigned to a variable 'X', which is then used to set the message PIN. The loop continues to send off messages until all the items in the array have been processed.

```
sms.MsgPin = X("mobilenum")
```

For each message sent, its status, confirmation of delivery or error report is displayed to the user.

3.10.3   SMS to All

An option to send a message to the entire database is also presented on 'Results.asp'. To achieve this a database connection is first opened and an SQL statement selects all mobile numbers from the 'Employee' table:

```
Set Connect = Server.CreateObject("ADODB.Recordset")

Connect.Open "SELECT mobilenum FROM employee", "diageo"
```

These mobile numbers are placed into an array:

```
Dim aTable1Values
aTable1Values = Connect.GetRows()
```

And for each element in the array a message is sent off.

3.11 SMS Validation

To ensure that a message is sent successfully, Client-side VBScript validation is employed. Subsequently a message cannot be transmitted to the SMSC unless the text-area used to compose messages contains text. The content of this text-area is first requested and checked. If it contains an empty string the user is asked to return and compose a message.

```
if request("msg")= ""  then
response.write ("<center><font face=Arial size=2
color=#990033>Please enter a Text Message <P>")
response.write ("<A Href=javascript:history.go(-1)> Go Back </A>")
response.end
end if
```

3.12 User Guide

The first screen that a user is presented with is illustrated in Figure 50. For this login process there are two possible outcomes. Either the user enters his/her details correctly and may proceed (see Figure 51) or the user enters an incorrect login (see Figure 52).

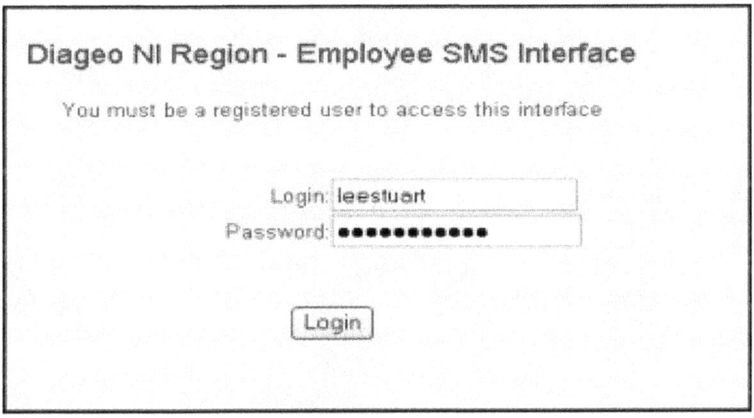

Diageo NI Region - Employee SMS Interface
You must be a registered user to access this interface
Login: leestuart
Password:
Login

Figure 50: SMS Login Screen

Diageo NI Region - Employee SMS Interface
You must be a registered user to access this interface
Login successful - Proceed

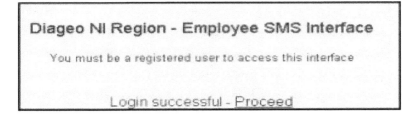

Figure 51: A successful Login

Or a recognized login and password is not given and the user may go no further:

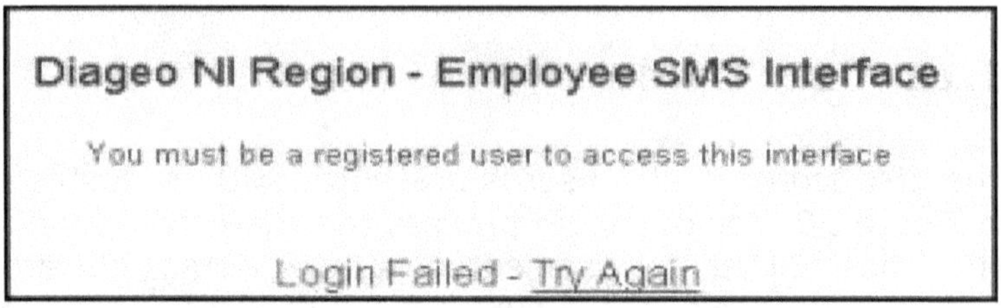

Figure 52: An unsuccessful Login

Upon reaching the homepage, the user has the options to go to three different pages, each link being tested to guarantee access to all parts of the interface.

3.12.1 Adding an Employee

To successfully add a new employee to the database, the user must proceed to the 'Add Employee' page (see Figure 53) and submit the employee details of first name, surname, mobile number, job title and region:

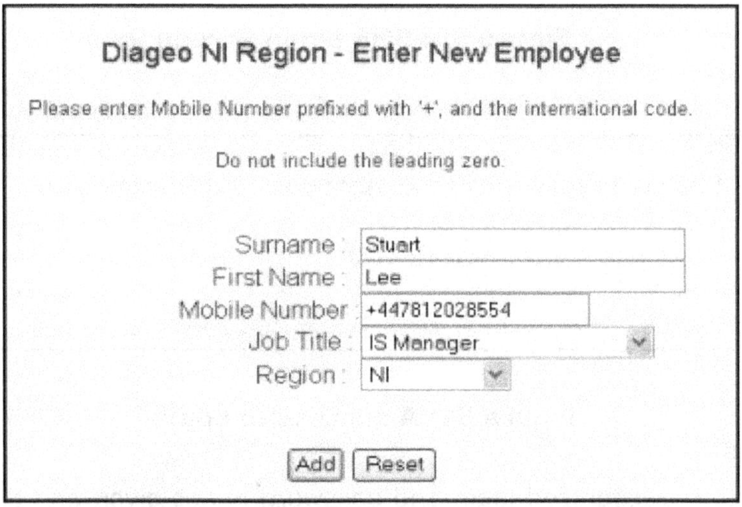

Figure 53: Adding an employee's details

Subsequently the submitted details are presented to the user as in Figure 54.

Figure 54: Employee Details added to the Database

An examination of the database concludes that the new details were successfully added as illustrated in Figure 55.

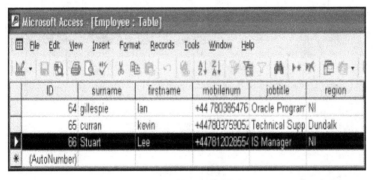

Figure 55: Details added to Database

When the user attempts to submit employee details to the database with incomplete fields, the user is alerted to complete the field left blank (see Figure 56).

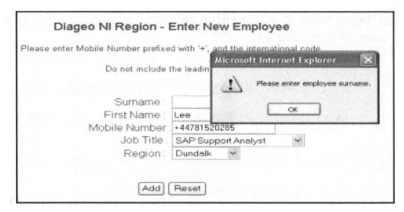

Figure 56: Validation of employee addition

To ensure a valid mobile number is entered, JavaScript validation is also used to limit the characters that can be entered to 0,1,2,3,4,5,6,7,8,9 and '+' (See Figure 57).

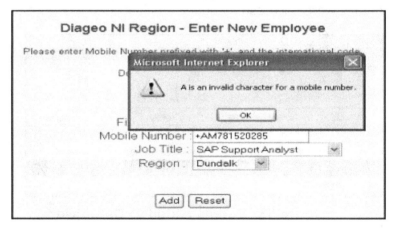

Figure 57: Validating characters for a mobile no.

3.12.2 Searching

The SQL statement that produces the results of a search had to be tested extensively to determine whether or not it could produce the correct responses to a user's query. A search by entering all details was found to display the correct result (see Figure 58).

Figure 58: Searching for an employee

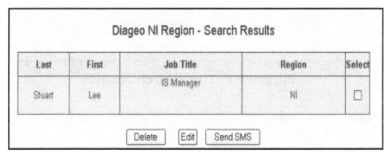

Figure 59: The search results

A search by surname alone, and then by mobile number alone also produces the same results (see Figure 59).

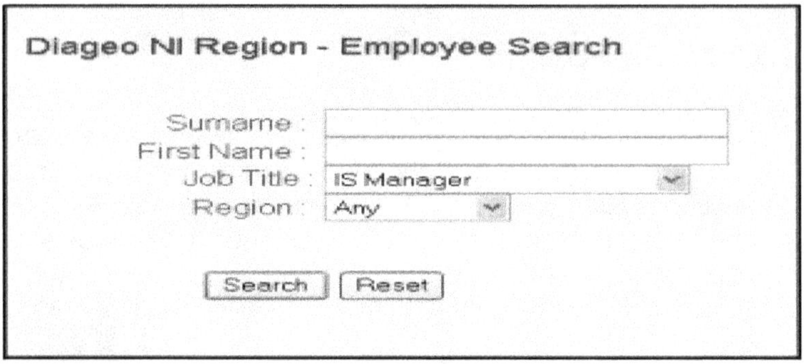

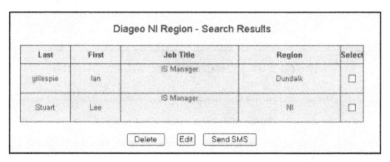

Figure 60: Searching for specific job title persons

Groups can be searched for such as for all employees with a certain job title (see Figure 60).

Last	First	Job Title	Region	Select
gillespie	Ian	IS Manager	Dundalk	☐
Stuart	Lee	IS Manager	NI	☐

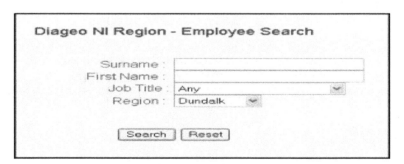

Figure 61: The search results

Those in a particular region can be retrieved (see Figure 62).

Figure 62: Searching by region.

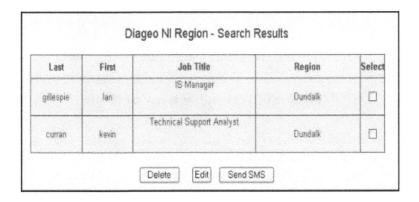

Figure 63: The Search results

3.12.3 Deleting Employees

With deletion, a safeguard is required to make certain that an accidental and irreversible erasing of data does not occur. Therefore JavaScript was employed to ensure that the user is requested for confirmation, prior to permanent deletion (see Figure 64).

Figure 64: Prompt to confirm deletion

Confirmation of deletion and how many records have been deleted is also an important user consideration (see Figure 65).

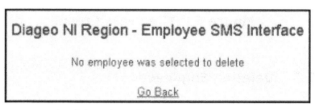

Figure 65: Feedback for deletion

Client-side VBScript is used to prompt the user should he/she not select an employee to delete as shown in Figure 66.

Figure 66: Prompt -no employee selected

3.12.4   Editing an Employee

When an employee is selected for editing, his/her details are displayed in a form format as shown in Figure 67).

Figure 67: Editing an employee

When the user is finished editing, they hit 'update' to send the reviewed employee details to the database shown in Figure 68.

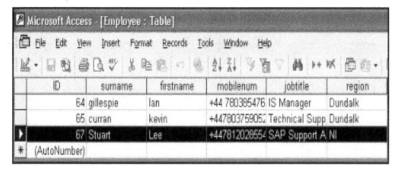

Figure 68: The updated employee details.

Since it is only possible to edit one employee at a time, the user must be informed of the need to select only one. This is achieved using VBScript as shown in Figure 69.

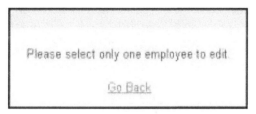

Figure 69: Only 1 employee is selected for editing

Validation must also exist to make sure that if no employee is selected the user is made aware as shown in Figure 70.

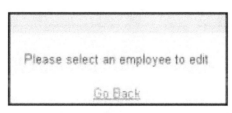

Figure 70: Ensuring at least 1 employee selected

3.12.5 Sending a Manual SMS

In order to send a manual SMS the user must first enter the desired recipient mobile number, followed by a text message and hit 'send' as shown in Figure 75.

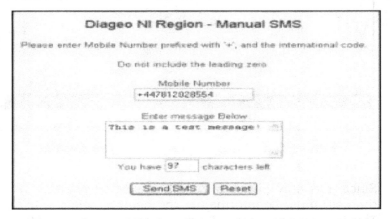

Figure 71: Sending a manual SMS

Confirmation of a successful send is returned from the SMSC as illustrated in Figure 72.

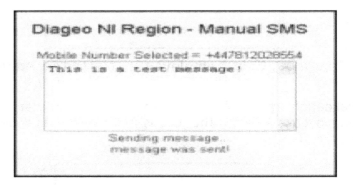

Figure 72: Confirmation of successful send

To prevent costly faults when sending an SMS, JavaScript is used to make sure a mobile number and message have been entered as shown in Figure 73.

Figure 73: Ensuring a mobile no. is entered

The same validation to ensure correct mobile number characters is also employed as shown in Figure 74.

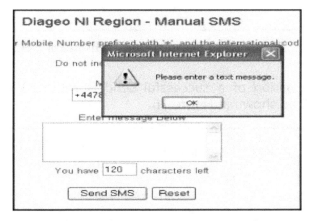

Figure 74: Ensuring a text-message is entered

3.12.6 Sending an Individual SMS

Firstly the desired recipient is selected from the results of a search, and a message composed as shown in Figure 75.

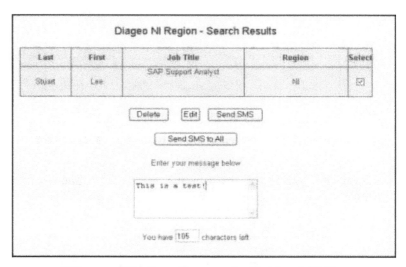

Figure 75: Sending an individual SMS

Confirmation of a successful send is returned from the SMSC as shown in Figure 76.

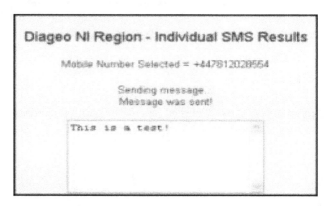

Figure 76: Confirmation of a successful send

3.12.7 Sending a Group SMS

All the intended recipients are selected from the search results, and a message is composed as shown in Figure 77.

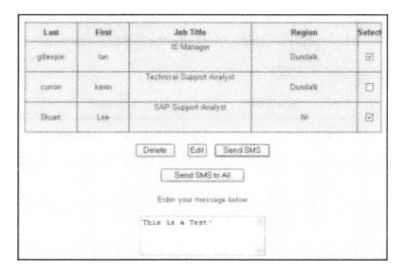

Figure 77: Selecting employees & composing SMS

Confirmation of all sent messages is returned to the user (see Figure 78).

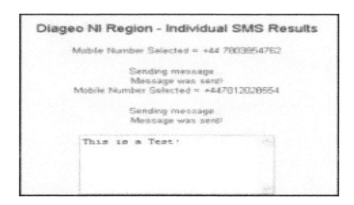

Figure 78: Confirmation of sent group message

Client-side VBScript ensures that a message cannot be sent unless employees are selected and a message composed as shown in Figure 79.

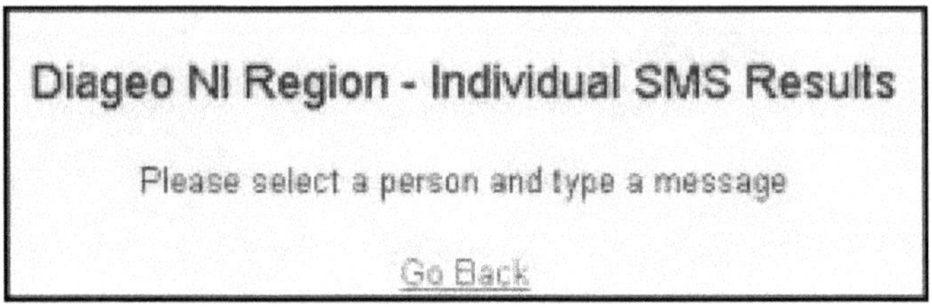

Diageo NI Region - Individual SMS Results

Please select a person and type a message

Go Back

Figure 79: Ensuring an employee selected

3.12.8   Sending a SMS to All

On the 'Results' page a message is composed and the user hits 'SMS to All' as shown in Figure 80.

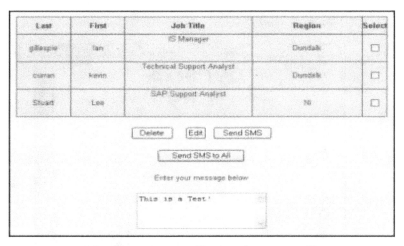

Figure 80: Sending a SMS to All

Confirmation of all sent messages is returned to the user (see Figure 81).

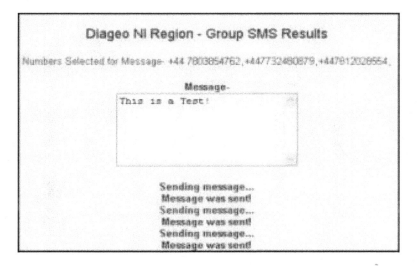

Figure 81: Confirmation of a send to all

3.12.9 Message Delivery

For testing purposes, Simplewire provide the developer with a virtual mobile number to ensure messages are arriving. Messages sent may then be viewed online (See Figure 82 and Figure 83).

Figure 82: Message arrival at Virtual Mobile

Figure 83: How the service may be used

3.13 Conclusion

The system presented here is fully functional. It is available for download from http://www.infm.ulst.ac.uk/~kevin/sms-asp.zip for non-commercial use.

The goal of a cost effective and time saving corporate SMS communication tool has been achieved. The fact that SMS is a rapidly growing technology means that the system will not become a dated application anytime in the near future; rather it may well be used as an example of how the technology can be applied for the benefit of the working environment. The system requires no installation of any software at the client-end, but rather can be used from any PC throughout the workplace to ensure communication can be achieved from anywhere, at any time. Such portability is useful in a working environment.

Students wishing to extend the application for an undergraduate project could do so in a number of ways such as:

- A future feature of the interface could be that of 2-way messaging, where employees could return an acknowledgement message to the user's desktop from their mobile phone. The Simplewire platform does support this technology, although it is not yet a feature. The capability is carrier dependent, and due to the low number of networks currently supporting the service is not yet a viable option. As the technology is taken on by more and more carriers, the system will hopefully be adapted to allow the returning of messages.

- Another proposed feature for the system could be the ability to use SMS to monitor the networks/systems as well as contact the employees who administrate them. Network crashes cost Companies enormous revenue each year and take up valuable employee time. An automatic signal such as an SMS to the IS manager would mean immediate detection and a simpler repair of crashed systems.

- With regards to database technologies, the system could eventually employ Microsoft SQL Server 2000 as its back-end database. Although Access was perfectly suited for the purposes of the project, SQL Server allows for a greater batch size and range of features, and is considered a more professional product.

Should the product become a permanent feature in a working environment, then it would be would be advisable to take the system off IIS and integrate it into the company's own infrastructure. This would likely mean a redesign of the pages themselves, with the database connectivity coding replaced with a language such as PERL or PHP.

4 Multimedia Messaging Service

"Multimedia Messaging Service (MMS) is a messaging service for the mobile environment, standardised by the WAP Forum and the 3rd Generation Partnership Program (3GPP)" [NokPress]. For the mobile user, MMS is similar to Short Message Service (SMS) - it provides automatic, immediate delivery of user-created content from mobile to mobile. MMS allows for the messages to be sent to both mobile numbers and e-mail addresses. This addressing feature is beneficial for MMS messaging to users who may not have an MMS capable handset. MMS messages can still be sent to non MMS capable handsets, however, the user will not be able to view the message on their mobile. Instead the user will be sent an SMS pointing to a URL address where they can view the message. In addition to the text that can be sent by SMS, MMS messages can contain images, voice, audio and later in development, video clips and presentation information as shown in

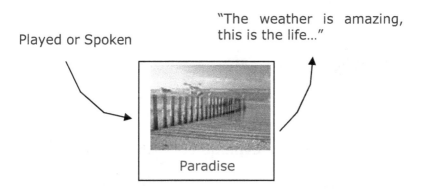

Figure 84: Message with Multimedia Content

An MMS message is a multimedia presentation in a single entry-it is not a text file with attachments. It can, for example, be a photo or picture postcard annotated with text and/or an audio clip, a synchronized playback of audio, text, photo or, in the near future, a video emulating a free-running presentation or a video clip. It

117

can also simply be a drawing combined with text. MMS is bearer independent and is not limited to only GSM (Global System for Mobile communications) or WCDMA (Wideband code-division multiple access) networks. MMS does not use the WAP browser in any way. The MMS application is a messaging application, not a browsing application. Therefore it requires its own user interface, just as SMS does. "Mobile phones have become an everyday accessory for hundreds of millions of people and they are also increasingly being used as the one and only means of personal voice telecommunication." [Ericevo] Three generations of mobile phones have emerged so far. Each successive generation has shown to be more flexible and reliable than the previous. This can be seen in Figure 85:

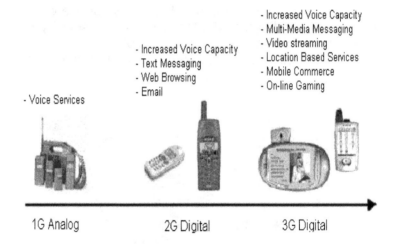

Figure 85: Evolution of mobile devices

4.1.1 "1G"

1G (first generation) mobile phones were introduced in the late 1970s/early 1980s and at the time represented a massive leap in mobile communication. The 1G devices only provided analog voice services, however, at the time "markets in the developed economies were not really asking for much more" [NancyGl].

118

4.1.2 "2G"

Advances in technology brought digital transmission to mobile communications. 2G (second generation) mobile technology made use of these advances and was able to improve transmission quality, system capacity and coverage. The technology used circuit-based, digital networks. Since 2G networks are digital, they are capable of carrying data transmissions, with speeds up to 10Kbps. The three standards involved in 2G networks are Time Division Multiple Access (TDMA), Code Division Multiple Access (CDMA) in America and Global System for Mobile (GSM) used in both America and Europe.

4.1.3 "2.5G"

"2.5" is an acronym which represents various technology upgrades to the existing 2G mobile networks. These upgrades include increasing the number of users a network can service, and boosting data transmission speeds to 140Kbps. 2.5G technology upgrades are designed to be overlaid on top of 2G networks with minimal additional infrastructure. An example of these technologies is General Packet Radio Service (GPRS), which allows for data to be transmitted over the network at speeds up to 140kps. "General Packet Radio Service (GPRS) enabled networks offer 'always-on', higher capacity, Internet-based content and packet-based data services. This enables services such as colour Internet browsing, e-mail on the move, powerful visual communications, multimedia messages and location-based services" [GSMgprs]. The introduction of 2.5G makes it possible for today's mobile operators to gain vital business and market experience by providing, high speed mobile data services. It also gives users a feel for the possibilities of 3G.

4.1.4 "3G"

"Tomorrow's information society will be characterised by a vastly increased worldwide market for users of mobile communications, providing businesses and consumers with a new world of media-rich information and entertainment services, spanning voice, video and high-speed Internet access, wherever they are in the world."

"3G will support far more users than today's networks and will offer data transmission speeds far in excess of today's second-generation systems. In fully mobile environments these speeds will reach up to 384kbits/sec; around forty times that possible today over current second-generation networks like GSM. In low mobility applications -- inside buildings for instance -- the comparisons become more dramatic still. At speeds of up to 2Mbit/sec, 3G will allow users to download complex graphics files, full motion video clips, and more, in seconds rather than minutes or even hours." [3Gevo] With these data rates, 3G will have a vital role to play within the office environment. "3G will facilitate high-speed access to corporate networks and intranets for office-bound workers" [3Gevo]. A major strength of 3G is its wireless high-speed access to the Internet, allowing super-fast downloads, providing the ability to play networked games and much more. Unrestricted by a fixed line connection to the Internet, users will be able to do the things they currently do on the Internet, on their mobile. Imagine being able to check train times from your phone when travelling overseas and perhaps even book a ticket from your phone. The boundaries are vast.

Speed aside, 3G will introduce new and better services, with more coverage, for more users. High-quality voice services will become cheaper. "The added appeal of 3G networks is that they will offer a high level of interworking with 2G operators to enable new players to meet their coverage obligations, so everybody in the operator community can continue to benefit from the continuing growth of the mobile market over the next several years" [3Gevo]. The potential for 3G is huge. The many services 3G will make available are expected to not only result in a corporate revolution but also a consumer revolution. Mobile users will benefit from more interactive and personalised applications for their phones, which in turn could significantly improve their lifestyles and the way they conduct business.

4.2 Multimedia Messaging Service

The main target area for MMS is mobile-to-mobile traffic. Because there is always the possibility of the receiving mobile not being able to receive a message, due to reasons such as an empty battery or poor network coverage, there is a new network element called the Multimedia Messaging Service Centre (MMSC). The MMSC is needed for storing MMS messages until the receiving phone is reached. It also hosts a number of interfaces to connecting networks and an API (Application Programming Interface) to enable delivery of value-added services and network interconnection to e-mail.

MMS standards do not state any specific content format for MMS messages. Instead, MMS messages are encapsulated in a standard way, so that the receiving party can identify content formats it does not support, and deal with them in a controlled manner. The following media types are recommended by the standard: JPEG, GIF, text, AMR voice and some other less-important formats. To achieve interoperability, a minimum set of content types to be supported by a MMS phone has been agreed by Nokia and some other manufacturers. Also due to interoperability reasons, a maximum 'MMS message' size has not been set. This has been done to avoid the SMS dilemma, of putting character limits on the messages. The message size is dependent on implementation and operator preferences. Some operators may want to set a message size limit for billing purposes. Some estimates so far, have been that an initial message size will range between 30kB and 100kB. The mobile network operator controls MMS charging. Orange[10] is charging 40p per message or bundles can be bought at 10 messages for £ 3. T-mobile[11] are charging 35p per message and bundles of 10 can be bought for £ 2.50 (25p per message) up to bundles of 50 for £ 10.50 (21p per message).

---

[10] www.orange.co.uk
[11] www.t-mobile.co.uk

4.2.1 MMS Transcoding

The process of encapsulating the MMS message content in a standard way is called transcoding. Essentially what happens is that the content is tailored before it arrives at the mobile. Transcoding systems can adapt video, images, audio and text to the individual constraints of different devices. They summarise, translate and convert the content into the MMS format. For example, one mobile may have a bigger screen than another or one supports GIF and the other supports only JPEG. These scenarios need to able to be adapted to and transcoding succeeds in doing this. Transcoding ensures interoperability, meaning that the MMS message will look as the sender expects it to. Without good interoperability, the user experience would be nullified. When a picture or voice clip is sent via MMS and it doesn't appear or sound as expected, then the user is less likely to use MMS again. With this, interoperability is a must for MMS. Transcoding is important not just for interoperability reasons, but also due to the current bandwidth limitations. Downloading images and movies onto an MMS mobile may take a few minutes, which may not be acceptable at times. Transcoding reduces file size while optimising them and enables the user experience to be maximised due to minimal downloading times.

4.2.2 MMS Protocol

MMS is a store-and-forward protocol. Messages are stored on the MMSC. Using WAP Push the recipient receives a notification message (basically an SMS message) from the message centre. "The notification message triggers the receiving terminal to retrieve the message automatically (or depending on filters defined by the user) using the WAP GET command. This allows the receipt of the message to be transparent to the user, as is the case with SMS." MMS uses Internet protocols like MIME (Multipurpose Internet Mail Extension) and SMTP (Simple Message Transfer Protocol) for access to the Multimedia Messaging Service Environment (MMSE). Initial MMS implementations will be based on enhanced WAP protocols (WAP MMS encapsulation), however, later MMS versions will also support non-WAP, standard internet protocols for communication between terminal and MMS relay, such as HTTP (Hypertext Transfer Protocol) over TCP/IP (Transmission Control Protocol on top of the Internet Protocol)

4.3 Sending an MMS Message

The 'basic' concept of sending an MMS message is the same as that of sending an SMS message:

- The message sender addresses the multimedia message to the receiver.
- The mobile contains information about the MMSC (MMS Centre), and the message is sent there.
- MMSC attempts to forward the message to the receiver.

If for some reason the receiver is unreachable, the MMSC stores the message for a time, and if possible, delivers the message later. If the message cannot be delivered within a certain time frame, it is eventually discarded.

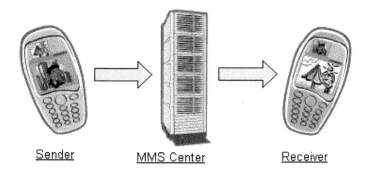

Sender   MMS Center   Receiver

Figure 86: Sending an MMS message

It is important to note that the MMSC does not directly try to send the message to the receiver, what it does is send a notification message telling the receiver that a message is waiting. Depending on the mobile settings, the message may be fetched immediately, held off until the user wants, or discarded completely. If automatic retrieval is set on the mobile, the user is only notified when the entire message has been delivered. Below in Figure 87, is a more detailed explanation of sending an MMS message.

124

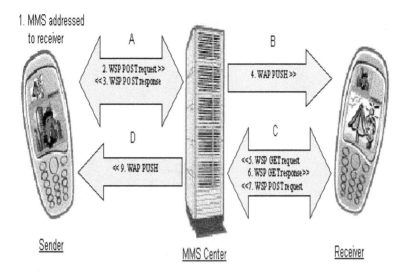

Figure 87: Sending an MMS message

Figure 87 can be broken up into the following steps.

- The message originator addresses the message to the receiver.
- The mobile contains information about the MMSC, initiates a WAP connection (CSD/GPRS), and sends the message as the content of a WSP POST.
- MMSC accepts message, and responds to originator over same WAP connection. Originator's terminal indicates "message sent".
- MMSC uses WAP PUSH to attempt to send an indication message to the receiver.
- Presuming receiver's terminal is set to accept MMSs, it initiates a WAP connection (CSD/GPRS), and uses WSP GET to retrieve the MMS message from the MMSC.
- MMS message is sent to receiver as content of a WSP GET RESPONSE over same WAP connection. Receiver's terminal indicates "message received".
- Receiver's terminal acknowledges receipt with WSP POST message, still over same WAP connection.
- MMSC user WAP PUSH to indicate to originator that message was delivered. Originator's terminal indicates "message delivered".

125

Figure 88 illustrates elements involved in an MMS.

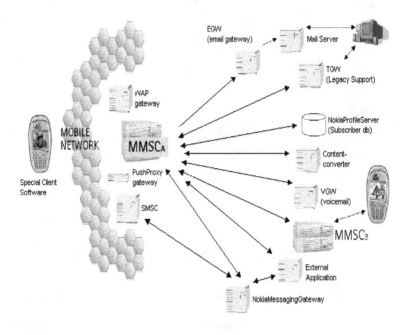

Figure 88: Elements in a Multimedia Messaging System

4.3.1 E-mail server/gateway

For MMS-message delivery to e-mail addresses, the MMSC must be able to communicate with existing mail servers, more than likely using SMTP (Simple Mail Transfer Protocol) protocol. Nokia's solution has been to create an E-mail Gateway (EGW), which lies between the MMSC and the e-mail server.

4.3.2 Legacy Support

In order to support non-MMS capable mobiles, Nokia have created a Terminal Gateway (TGW) to work as a legacy-messaging server. It works by storing the MMS message in its own storage, and then it sends an SMS message to the MMS message's intended receiver, with a URL pointing to where the message can be viewed.

4.3.3 Subscriber Database

The principle behind the subscriber database is to have a database of subscriber profiles to help when deciding what type of content to deliver. For example, if A sends B an MMS message, the MMSC can determine via the database, that B does not have an MMS capable mobile, and send the message directly to the TGW, as described above. Nokia have implemented this concept by allowing subscribers to be able to set up message receipt options, e.g. all incoming messages can also be sent to a mailbox.

4.3.4 Content Converter

An example may be that one user may send another user an image in a format that is not supported by their terminal. The MMSC determines this from the subscriber database, and sends the image to a content converting application. This application converts the image to a format that is supported by the user's terminal and sends it forward to them.

4.3.5 Voicemail

Instead of receiving a text message indicating that there is a voice message stored, the voice message is now encapsulated in an MMS message and sent directly to the phone.

4.4 Comparison between SMS and MMS

The Short Messaging Service (SMS) is the dominant messaging service in the mobile world at present, with tens of billions of SMS messages sent and received every month globally. As seen in Table 7 below, MMS is predicted to tap into this market and indeed eclipse it over the coming years. SMS will still remain one of common ways people will communicate, however, MMS's richness of communication is set to become the dominant form of messaging in the near future.

FEATURE	SMS	MMS
Store and Forward (non real time)	Yes	Yes
Confirmation of message delivery	Yes	Yes
Communications Type	Person to person	Application to Person Person to person
Media supported	Text plus binary	Multiple-Text, images, Video
Protocols	SMS specific e.g. SMPP	WAP and general Internet e.g. MIME, HTTP, SMTP
Configuration	Simple telephone number	Diverse Parameters
Platforms	SMS Centre	MMS Relay plus others
Principle Applications	Simple person to person	Still images, person to person, server based MMS services e.g. video news
User behaviour	Discreet	Indiscrete

Table 7: Comparison between SMS and MMS

Both SMS and MMS are non-real time services, meaning that both must pass through an intermediate platform on route to the mobile. They pass through the likes of an SMS centre or an MMS Relay. Both give the sender confirmation of delivery, allowing the sender to know that the message sent was successfully delivered.

128

4.4.1 Media Supported

The SMS support text and binary as media compared with MMS supporting media ranging from text to images to sound to video, and also a combination of these media. This clearly shows the power of MMS and the possibilities of communications available to the user.

4.4.2 Delivery Mechanism

The signalling channel over which SMS messages are sent and received is an additional transport mechanism on GSM networks, over and above the radio channels themselves. Similar in principle to the hard shoulder on the motorway, it runs parallel to the traffic lanes themselves. Instead of running parallel to the traffic lanes, multimedia messages will be transmitted over the traffic lanes themselves, alongside the voice data and other data being transported. 3G's high capacity will mean that the different traffic types can share the traffic lanes without the chance of congestion.

4.4.3 Protocols

Short Message Peer to Peer (SMPP) has become the standard SMSC interface protocol in recent years. It is also likely to be used for some MMS interfaces. "MMS uses standard internet protocols such as MIME (Multipurpose Internet Mail Extension) and SMTP (Simple Message Transfer Protocol) for access to the Multimedia Messaging Service Environment (MMSE)." [Mmsdata]

4.4.4 Configuration

SMS is very easy to use. There are no special numbers to remember in order to send a message. The sender just enters the recipient's mobile number.   MMS message sending is much more complex than SMS message sending. "In the initial implementation of MMS using WAP, WAP Push is used such that concatenated SMS messages are used to transport the notification data (sender, size, retrieval URL, etc.) encapsulated in a WAP Push data unit. The 3GPP IP-based implementation proposal for MMS does not include SMS notification – it assumes a pure HTTP payload between the terminal and the relay" [Mmsdata]. This will require the user to enter more details about the content of the messages being sent.

4.4.5 Platforms

The SMS Centre is at the core of the SMS service, with all short messages of any type passing through one, on route to and from mobile phones. This being so means that there is only one platform type dominating SMS. MMS on the other hand has many key platforms within its environment, MMSE – including the MMS Centre (combination of MMS Relay and the MMS message store), the MMS User Database and other platforms including existing platforms such as the SMSC, voice mail platforms and the like.

4.4.6 Applications

The vast majority of SMS traffic accounted for is simple person to person messaging in which people send messages such as "How's it going?." MMS allows for more advanced applications. Screen savers, photos, etc., can to be sent from Internet sites.

4.4.7 User Behaviour

The sending of SMS can be a very discreet operation that can take place virtually anywhere, for example, in an office meeting without disturbing anyone. MMS is completely different, in that, sending MMS messages will draw attention to the sender, for example, if the user is taking a picture using a built in camera in the phone.

4.5 Predicted Growth for MMS

The evolution of SMS to MMS on mobile handsets will have a huge impact on the way mobile users communicate in the near future. Moving from sending simple text messages through a monochrome mobile handset to being able to send images, video, audio and data to MMS-enabled mobile phones will enrich the user's experience and enjoyment. "Unlike SMS, MMS provides an excellent platform for customers, with a colourful, user-friendly application interface." [Sharp] It is no surprise, then, that the telecommunications industry seeks to revolutionise messaging by enhancing its robustness and delivering on a promise to bring the next generation of communications to mobile consumers. "Today, analysts estimate that more than 62 billion SMS messages will be sent worldwide on a monthly basis in 2002. That translates into a little more than 5.7 billion euros in transaction revenue per month." [Sharp] One research organisation, Mobile Streams, recently published forecasts for the number of monthly messages and revenue for SMS and MMS, see Figure 89:

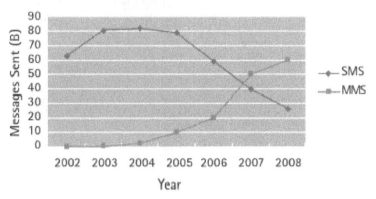

Figure 89: Global MMS Monthly Market forecast[12]

---

[12] http://www.dhtml-zone.com/Nokia/Article/6969

From this graph above, we can see that MMS traffic is expected to exceed SMS sometime in 2007. "Data excludes Japan. (Source: Mobile Streams, 2001)" [Sharp]

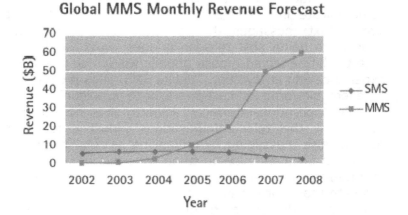

Figure 90: Global MMS monthly revenue forecast[13]

From Figure 90, we can see that revenue from MMS is expected to exceed revenue from SMS around mid 2004, with the higher 'revenue per message' being the reason. he chart below shows the predicted revenue from mobile messaging in Europe up until 2006. It is estimated that in 2006, MMS revenue will be worth roughly £6 billion, and the total messaging revenue worth £30 billion. "(Source: The Yankee Group, 2002)" [Sharp]

---

[13] http://www.dhtml-zone.com/Nokia/Article/6969

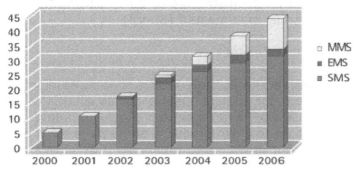

Figure 91: Messaging revenue in Europe, 2000-06[4]

It can be seen from Figure 91, that the revenue to be earned through mobile messaging is enormous. There are many benefits for all incorporated in the mobile environment. These include:

For Mobile Users:

- Messaging is the modern way to communicate. It's instant, location independent, and personal.
- MMS allows users to enrich the messages they send with images and sound, thus satisfying users desires for rich personal communication.
- MMS is very flexible, in that it can be used for all types of mobile phones and can be sent to e-mail addresses.

For Operators:

- MMS provides a natural path to continual growth. This new service beyond voice communication allows operators to increase free airtimes, service differentiation and customer loyalty.
- "As MMS is bearer independent, it leverages GPRS (General Packet Radio Service) and WCDMA (Wideband code-division multiple access) investments by providing a mass-market application for them and adding value to the utilisation of infrastructure. Early adaptors can

133

secure a strong position and accumulate the required competencies to be leaders in the era of personal multimedia." [Sharp]

For Content Providers:

- MMS facilitates three factors that boost information value for phone users: personalisation, time-sensitivity and mobility. Applying these three factors to their products and services will enable content providers to maximise their attractiveness to mobile users.
- MMS is fast, personal, auditive and visual, so providing content for such a service is a big opportunity as it's popularity is set to grow enormously over the next decade.

For Advertisers:

- MMS's capabilities open a direct link between advertiser and customers. Customers can now receive online marketing messages with the possibility of transactions over the mobile.

For Developers:

- MMS will generate a need for developers across a broad range of areas, from creating interesting content to storage services for downloading to aggregation software.

MMS message services will be used for a broad spectrum of uses, such as:

- Information services – local content like traffic reports, finance, weather forecasts, e-mail delivery...
- Entertainment & Personalisation services – animated wallpaper images, collector cards, games, music & video samples...
- Communication – MMS chat, dating services
- MMS as conduit – sending various media over MMS

5 An MMS Application

Functional requirements describe the services the system has to offer. Each description should use natural language. Technical jargon should be avoided. Simple diagrams should be drawn for each requirement. These diagrams should be easily understood by customers, users, and management. The functional requirements for this system are sub-divided into two sections, as there are two clear areas of functionality dealt with, namely sending an MMS message from the application and Receiving an MMS message on an MMS-capable mobile phone. The functional requirements for this generic MMS system presented here are:

- An easy to use Graphical User Interface (GUI) that may be created adhering to certain design principles
- The system shall store the following information about each message clip: size, format, media, etc.
- The system will enable MMS message sending to mobile phones
- The system shall provide searching and browsing access to general customers. They shall see a select subset of the overall MMS database.
- The system shall provide advanced searching, browsing, and editing functionalities to customers and developers. This will require differing levels of access and controls.
- The system shall validate user selected content and sending parameters (mobile number or email address).

The functional requirements for sending an MMS message are:

- Select the message content from its stored location,
- Send message to mobile number or email address,
- Ability when sending message, to send to one of the 10 most used numbers or addresses,
- Feedback from the application telling user if message has been sent successfully.

The functional requirements for retrieving an MMS message are:

- User will be able to see the message in their inbox, each represented by the user who sent the message and maybe the subject.
- With the list of inbox messages displayed, the user is able to view more details on any particular message, e.g. subject, time sent, message size, number, type and size of components of message.
- User should be able to view full content of message, e.g. images, sounds, and text.

Non-functional requirements describe constraints placed on the system and on the designers which may impact later phases such as the design e.g. cost, time scales, database performance, specific data representations, memory requirements and standards [Somvlle95]. These requirements are often prone to change as they are closely tied to hardware, an area where advances are happening very quickly. Non-functional requirements must also be worded in a way that can be verified quantitatively. Software developers tend to stress the importance of the functional requirements of an application more than the non-functional requirements during development. However, this may prove to be an inaccurate decision as in the case of this project it could lead to a perfectly designed User Interface while lacking the ability to provide users with results in 'real-time'. Due to the technological aspects employed and the requirement of a 'real-time' application within this project, a big emphasis has been placed on the non-functional requirements also. "If a real-time system does not meet its performance requirements, it may be completely useless" [Somvlle95].

The following have been identified as the key non-functional requirements that are necessary to ensure that an MMS application is both technically and fundamentally sound.

- **Performance & Efficiency** - The need for the application to deliver messages quickly with little delay and to have the ability to automatically receive updated logs.

- **Throughput Capability** – The application must be capable of handling X number of messages in a given period.

- **Response Time** – The application must be capable of responding to user requests (e.g. for image/text or audio files) with a minimal delay.

- **Portability** - The system must be platform independent, which allows a user to use any computer operating system or computer architecture to run the desired Multimedia Messaging Application.

- **Flexibility** - The application must be capable of dealing with both requests and replies simultaneously.

- **Scalability** - The application must be able to handle different types and sizes of images and be able to scale these to be viewable on the mobile device.

- **Feedback** – It must avoid errors and give good feedback if an error occurs.

The minimum hardware requirements are a PC equipped with an Intel Pentium 11 or faster processor (400 MHz or faster recommended), 128 MB or more recommended and at least 300 MB hard disk space. There is also a need for a MMS phone for testing.

With regards software, a combination of the following products creates a full MMS development environment:

- Nokia Developer's Suite for MMS
- Nokia Series 60 MMS SDK for Symbian OS
- Nokia MMSC EAIF emulator

- J2SE (Java 2 Platform, Standard Edition)

The MMS development environment allows for full testing of the application before use in the real market. Nokia Series 60 MMS SDK for Symbian OS emulator provides a preview capability for the created messages. Below is a screenshot of the emulator:

Figure 92: Nokia MMS SDK for Symbian OS emulator

The Nokia MMSC EAIF emulator allows viewing of MMS messages in the MMSC server External Application Interface (EAIF). It is a tool, which enables testing of applications without connection live to an MMSC. The emulator simulates the functionality of EAIF and with it correct functionality of applications can be verified. In the originating application case, the emulator receives the message from the application, validates that all the fields of the message are in correct format and returns the HTTP response with the corresponding success code to the application. The management functionality of the emulator provides tools for viewing the log of the emulator; viewing the HTTP responses the application is returning and viewing MMS message validation process. This functionality can be very helpful in case some problems exist.

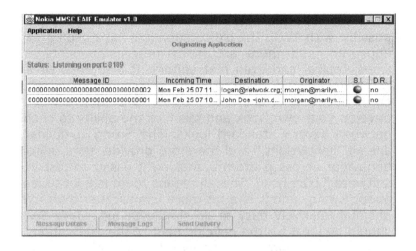

Figure 93: Nokia MMSC EAIF emulator[14]

To develop the application, JDK 1.3.0 or above is needed, available from J2SE on a free download from http://java.sun.com. "J2SE provides the essential compiler, tools, runtimes, and APIs for writing, deploying, and running applets and applications in the Java programming language." [Sun]. The application interface that to be developed will be created using Java Swing. Below is a brief explanation of Java Swing. The Java Swing interface will make use of the MMS Java Library provided as part of the 'Nokia Developer's Suite for MMS'. "The Swing toolkit is a fully-featured UI component library implemented entirely in the Java programming language. J2SE's javax.swing package uses the windowing functionality of AWT[15] and the rendering capabilities of Java 2D[16] to provide sophisticated and highly extensible UI components that comply with the JavaBeans™ [17] specification." [Swing].

"The Swing classes eliminate Java's biggest weakness: its relatively primitive user interface toolkit. Swing provides many new components and containers that allow you to

---

[14] http://www.forum.nokia.com/main/1,35452,1_2_7_1,00.html
[15] http://java.sun.com/products/jfc/#awt
[16] http://java.sun.com/products/jfc/#java2d
[17] http://java.sun.com/products/javabeans/

build sophisticated user interfaces, far beyond what was possible with AWT. The old components have been greatly improved, and there are many new components, like trees, tables, and even text editors. It also adds several completely new features to Java's user interface capabilities: drag-and-drop, undo, and the ability to develop your own "look and feel," or the ability to choose between several standard looks. The Swing components are all "lightweight," and therefore provide more uniform behaviour across platforms, making it easier to test your software." [Oreiljsw] This all means there is a lot to learn about Swing, and it is a lot more complicated than AWT, but still relatively easy to do simple things. Java Swing should be ideal for the development of the application, as it will be able to integrate easily with the MMS Java library provided as part of the development kit that will be used. The 'basic' concept of sending an MMS message will be the same as that of sending an SMS message as described previously. The message will be able to be sent to a mobile phone or an e-mail address.

Figure 94 presents a flow chart of the transcoding framework is shown giving an overview of the system's flow of control:

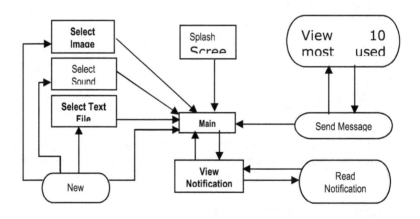

Figure 94: Multimedia Messaging Application

The system design can be represented using techniques from the Unified Modelling Language (UML). One of these techniques is 'use case modelling', which represents user interaction with the system. Figure 95 depicts a high-level use case diagram, which shows the highest level of interactions between user and system.

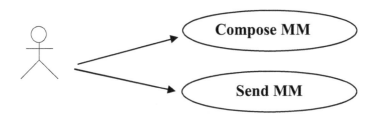

Figure 95: High-level use case diagram:

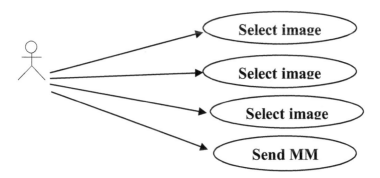

Figure 96: Elementary send message

To implement the functionality outlined earlier, the front end user interface, is implemented using Java Swing and its classes, and will make use of the MMS Java Library provided as part of the Nokia development environment. It will use the MMS Java Library classes to transcode the message into MMS format and deploy it to the mobile phone.

141

5.1 User Interface

The term 'Human Computer Interaction' (HCI) refers to the way a person experiences the computer, its application programmes, hardware components, output devices and functionality. It includes all aspects of the human's experience from the obvious ones of screen layout and selection options as well as input and output devices, reliability and accessibility [Shneid].

Over recent years, HCI is steadily growing in stature. One of the key concepts of HCI is usability. Usability comprises a number of factors, or questions that can be asked about a computer package, bearing in mind the type of user and the tasks for which it has been produced. These questions can provide some measure of how well the specified users can perform the desired activities with the system. The questions can be considered generally under headings such as:

- **Learnability** – How easy is it to learn how to use the system? How well are the learned skills retained over time?

- **Throughput** – How quickly can the tasks be performed (or, how many people might be needed to perform a task?), What is the user error-rate? How easily can user/system recover from errors?

- **Flexibility** – How suitable is the system for the expertise of the intended users? Can the system be customised to suit different ways of working and /or different levels of expertise?

- **Attitude** – What is the users' subjective satisfaction with the system?

It is essential when developing a system to identify potential users and how they will interact with the system. Software developers must pay close attention to interface design, as this is how the users will mainly interact with the system. In a nutshell, this means the user should not have to adapt to the interface; rather the interface should be intuitive and natural for the user to learn and to use. This project is focusing more on the technology behind the interface, although developing a user interface that can positively answer the questions above will result in an application with good usability.

The user interface was implemented using the Java Swing classes provided as part of the J2SE environment. The interface makes use of the Nokia MMS Java Library, which contains the classes needed to create MMS messages and to send messages to the MMSC. Experimenting with various layout managers that the swing classes offer helped when developing the main screen 'MMSApp.java'. The image selected for the top of the main screen blends in well with the other colours and the log panel at the bottom of the screen fits well into the application by telling the user what files they have selected and if the message was sent successfully.

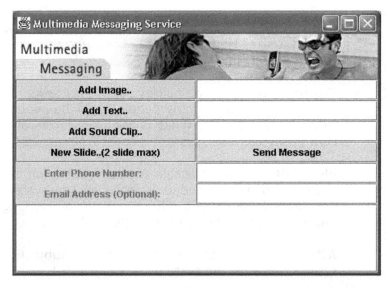

Figure 97: Application main screen

The main screen 'MMSApp.java' (see Figure 97) uses swings 'filechooser' class for when the image/text and audio buttons are pressed. Each filechooser was implemented differently. The image filechooser was coded such that it could display small thumbnail icons of the images, to enable the user to choose the image they wanted. Each of the filechoosers was implemented in a way that the type of files that could be selected from each differently. Only image files could be chosen from the image filechooser, only text files could be chosen from the text filechooser, and only audio files could be chosen from the audio filechooser. This also left no room for user error by selecting the wrong file type for a specific type of the message content. Once the content was selected, the 'MMSApp.java' class called the 'OringinatingApp.java' class and it passed in the message content to it. This class then built up the message in a container and added the necessary headers for sending the message, as will be described later.

5.2 MMS Message as a Container

The message content used in the application will contain a maximum of two of each of the types of media in the figure below.

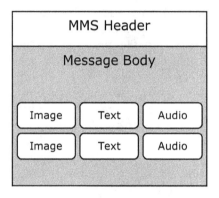

Figure 98: MMS Content structure

The MMS Protocol Data Unit (PDU) structure is specified by the WAP Forum in specification WAP-209-MMSEncapsulation [WapFrm]. Logically the MMS PDU consists of headers and a multipart message body. The message body may contain any content type and MIME multipart is used to represent and encode a wide variety of media types for transmission via multimedia messaging. The content type of the MMS PDU is application/vnd.wap.mms-message. Figure 99 depicts a conceptual model and an example of the encapsulation.

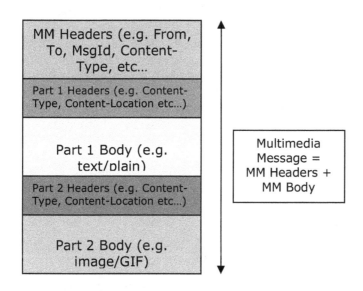

Figure 99: Structure of MMS PDU

Table 8 shows some of the mandatory headers needed for the sending of a multimedia message.

Name	Content	Comments
X-Mms-Message-Type	Message-type-value=m-send.req	Mandatory. Specifies the transaction type.
X-Mms-Transaction-ID	Transaction-id-value	Mandatory. A unique identifier for the message. Identifies the M-send.req and the corresponding reply only.
X-Mms-Version	MMS-version-value	Mandatory. The MMS version number.
From	From-value	Mandatory. Address of the message sender. This field must be present in a message delivered to a recipient.
Content-Type	Content-type-value	Mandatory. The content type of the message.

Table 8: Header fields of M-Send.req PDU

5.3 Originating Application

The application developed is called an originating application. This is an application that is the originating sources of messages. It sends OA (application-originated) messages. Other types of applications are terminating applications and filtering applications. Terminating applications are the applications in which messages are terminated.

They receive AT (application terminated) messages. Filtering applications receive a message from the MMS Centre, process the message, and then send the message (or status) back to the MMS Centre for further processing.

Filtering applications may:

- Modify the message (for example, content conversion).
- Process the message in some other way (for example, make a copy and forward the copy somewhere else).

On a general level the originating applications are responsible for:

- Message content creation/selection (text, images, audio, or combination of these)
- Message creation (M-Send.req header creation, content MIME encapsulation etc.)
- HTTP POST request creation (creation of HTTP headers and extension headers, insertion of the binary encoded MMS PDU to the body)
- HTTP POST request delivery over EAIF to MMSC

Originating applications submit the messages over the EAIF to the MMSC in HTTP POST requests. The M-Send.req MMS PDU is binary encoded and carried over the EAIF in the body of the HTTP POST request.

Table 9 shows the structure of a HTTP POST request containing the MMS PDU.

HTTP POST request from an originating application containing the M-Send.req
POST/HTTP/1.1 Host: mmsc.operator.com:80 Content-Type: application/vnd.wap.mms-message
CONTENT-LENGTH: 188
m-send.req

Table 9: POST request from originating app

The M-Send.req in the body of the POST request in the example above contains the following headers and the corresponding values:

> X-Mms-Message-Type: m-send-req
> X-Mms-Transaction_ID: 1884022032
> X-Mms-Version: 1.1
> From: +123333333333/TYPE=PLMN
> To: +123455555555/TYPE=PLMN
> Subject: This is a Multimedia Message
> Content-Type:
> application/vnd.wap.multipart.mixed

Once the MMSC has received and interpreted the HTTP POST request, it sends a POST response indicating the status of the operation. The response consists of a status line containing three fields: HTTP version, status code, and textual description. The HTTP version indicates the version of the recipient's result to the sender's request. The description following the status code is just human-readable text that describes the status code. Optionally the response can contain also extension headers, which carry for example charging information. The following example contains a positive response indicating that the requested operation was successful.

Table 10 shows the HTTP response from MMSC to originating application. This response can be seen in the application when a message is sent from it.

HTTP response from MMSC to originating application
HTTP/1.1 204 No Content X-NOKIA-MMSC-Message-Id: 07zt5awVc3cAAGZSAAAAAQAAAAAIAAAA X-NOKIA-MMSC-Version: 1.1

Table 10: Response from MMSC to originating app

Taking all the above into account, below is a sample of OriginatingApp.java that was used to wrap the message in the appropriate headers and build up the content. 'OriginatingApp.java' made use of the MMS Java Library classes to encode the message into the MMS format for sending.

```
public OriginatingApp(File imageFileOne, File
textFileOne, File soundFileOne) {
        MMMessage mm = new MMMessage();
        SetMessage(mm);
        AddContents(mm, imageFileOne, textFileOne,
soundFileOne);
        MMEncoder encoder=new MMEncoder();
        encoder.setMessage(mm);
     try {
        encoder.encodeMessage();
        byte[] out = encoder.getMessage();
        MMSender sender = new MMSender();
        sender.setMMSCURL("http://127.0.0.1:8189");
        sender.addHeader("X-NOKIA-MMSC-Charging",
"100");
        MMResponse mmResponse = sender.send(out);
        System.out.println("Message sent to " +
sender.getMMSCURL());
        System.out.println("Response code: " +
mmResponse.getResponseCode() + " " +
mmResponse.getResponseMessage());
        }
    }
....
....
```

150

5.4 Sending a message to the MMSC

The Nokia MMSC EAIF is designed to be used with HTTP 1.1 and persistent connection mechanism. Using persistent connection mechanism means that once the HTTP connection between EAIF and the external application has been opened, several request/responses can be sent using the same connection. HTTP messages consist of two parts: HTTP headers and the message body. MMS Centre uses standard HTTP headers as well as some Nokia MMS Centre-specific HTTP extension headers. The HTTP headers may be in any order but they must precede the message body. Multimedia messages are sent in the HTTP message body, as in the figure below.

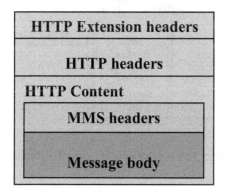

Figure 100: POST request containing the MMS PDU

In the MMS specific HTTP extension headers, the following information can be conveyed:

> Message-Id
> Message Status
> Charging Information
> Message recipient (To)
> Message sender (From)
> MMSC version

Some of the mandatory HTTP headers in the external application interface are:

Host, whether it is the MMSC or an application. E.g. mmsc.operator.com:80 or external.application.com: 80 Content-Type of the message body. In MMS, the content-type is application/vnd.wap.mms-message. Content-Length, indicates the length of the content in the message body. The application is an originating application that acts as a web client originating the multimedia messages. Correspondingly the MMSC is acting as a web server receiving the HTTP requests from the client (application). Figure 101 illustrates the roles of the application and Java classes.

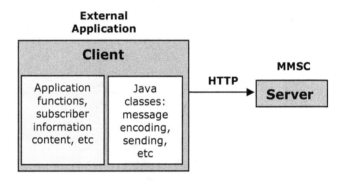

Figure 101: Java library in originating app case

When sending an MMS message to the MMSC, the example Java classes present how the following functions can be implemented, which helped when coding the application:

- Message encoding, according to MIME.
- Message delivery to the MMSC, over HTTP.

The java classes presented how to encapsulate the MMS content (images, text, etc.) using MIME and how to create and encode the whole MMS PDU containing the content in the body. After the message creation, the Java classes present how to insert the encoded message to the HTTP POST request and how to deliver the message over the EAIF to the MMSC.

5.5 MMS User Guide

Once the application is running on the main screen, if the user decides to try to send a message, before any content has been added to it, the following error message appears (see Figure 102).

Figure 102: Empty message content alert

When the user presses the 'Add Image..' button, the screen in Figure 103 is displayed. This was coded such that the next screen would show a small thumbnail image of the possible images and also that it only showed image files, so no other files can be selected by mistake.

Figure 103: File Chooser with thumbnail icon

This ensures that the correct types of files are added together to make up the message content. When adding a text file or sound clip, users can select only text or sound clips. If users attempt to create a new slide for more message content while there is no content in the first slide, the system displays an error message as in Figure 104.

Figure 104: New slide error alert

If a user attempts to add more than two slides to the message, the following alert is displayed to them (Figure 105). The user can replace the content in each slide but cannot add a third slide with new content.

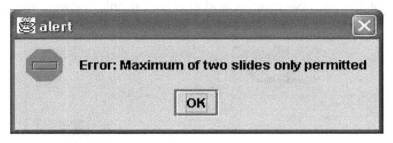

Figure 105: Two-slide maximum alert

When a file is attached, the textbox adjacent to the button gets updated with the file name, and the entire file path gets updated in the log at the bottom of the screen. This can be seen in Figure 106.

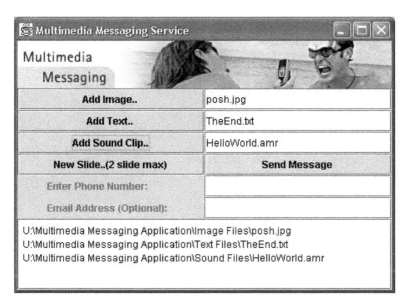

Figure 106: Main screen file details

At this stage if a user attempts to send the message, the system will throw up an error alert telling the user to enter a mobile number (see Figure 107).

Figure 107: No mobile number alert

The toolkit from Nokia provides the multimedia messaging service centre (MMSC) and the phone emulator. This enables the testing of message sending from the application to the phone emulator via the MMSC. Figure 108, Figure 109, Figure 110 and Figure 111 show some of the screenshots of the MMSC and information that it provides.

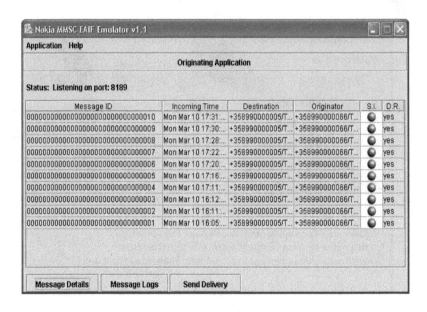

Figure 108: Nokia MMSC EAIF Emulator v1.1

Clicking on the message details button brings up the following screen.

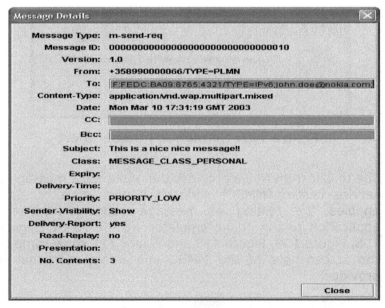

Figure 109: Message details screen

Clicking on the message logs screen brings up the following screen shown in Figure 110.

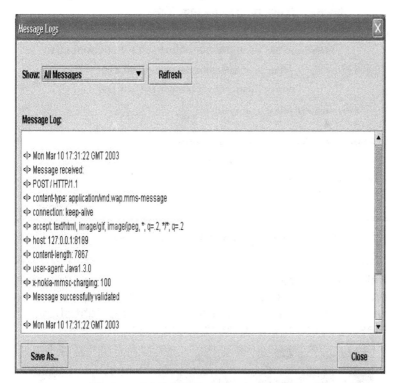

Figure 110: Message Log screen

Clicking on the send delivery button brings up the following screen shown in Figure 111.

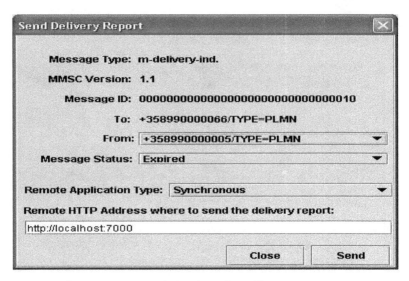

Figure 111: MMSC Send Delivery Report

Below in Figure 112 are two screen shots of the phone emulator. The screen shot on the left shows the inbox with the message in it and the one on the right shows the message with the picture of David Beckham.

Figure 112: Phone Emulator inbox and message

5.6 Conclusion

The aim of this chapter was to demonstrate a sample MMS application. The prototype (with code outlined in Appendices A, B, C, D, E, F & G) can transcode various media into correct format for sending as part of a multimedia message. As a result of being written in Java, the program can be executed on a number of different platforms without having to recompile the code.

There is much scope for future modification. Under-graduate students wishing to pursue a project in a related area could perhaps tackle some of the following additional functionality:

- Edit text files within the application – The application could incorporate some sort of text editor to allow the user not only to select saved text files, but to create and edit text files as these wish when creating content for the messages.

- Ability to record sound clips from the users' terminal and send as part of the message content .A voice recorder could be added to the application to save voice clips into the correct format for sending as part of the message content.

- User profiles could be implemented to allow different users to store their own content. This may also be implemented to permit a maximum number of messages to be sent per day.

- A personalised phone book containing mobile numbers and email addresses – The application could contain user phone books and email addresses, but may also allow for browsing over the internet to find certain phone numbers of email addresses. This browsing capability could also be used to find content for the messages.

- Application could become web-based – This would allow users to log on practically anywhere in the

world and sign into their own accounts' and create
and send messages over the web.

6 References

[Allamaraju01] Allamaraju, S. Professional Java E-Commerce, Wrox Press Ltd., Canada. pp. 823., 2001

[Arizcm]
http://arizonacommunity.com/articles/java_32001.shtml

[BCS98] The British Computer Society, 1998, A Glossary of Computing Terms, 9th Edition,   Longman

[Connolly02] Connolly, T and Begg, C. (2002). *Database Systems*. 3rd edition. London: Addison-Wesley.

[Copeland00] Copeland et Al. (2000). *Which Web Development Tool is Right for You?* IT Pro, March/April 2000, pp20-27.

[Ericevo]
http://learning.ericsson.net/eeonline/course_material/wc dma_systems/wcdma_systems_r1/articles/2g_to_3g_evol ution.shtml

[ForumNk] http://www.forum.nokia.com HOW TO CREATE MMS SERVICES, Version 3.2, 06-09-2002

[GSMgprs]
http://www.gsmworld.com/technology/gprs/index.shtml

[Hume01] Ron Hume. Short Message Services, *Dr. Dobb's Journal*, pp: 62-69, October 2001

[Mmsfaq] http://www.mobilemms.com/mmsfaq.asp

[Mmsdata]
http://www.mobilemms.com/sample_dataonmms.asp

[Mmstran]
http://www.mobilemms.com/sample_mmstranscoding.as p

[Mobiledata02] July 2002, UK Text message figure for June tops 1.3 billion. http://www.mda-mobiledata.org/resource/hottopics/sms.asp

[NancyGl] http://www.nancyglobal.com.futuresite.register.com/_wsn/page3.html

[NokPress] http://nokia-sia.com/nokia_apac/asia_pacific/nokia_insight_press_release/0,17289,409,00.html

[Northst01] Wholesale SMS. http://www.northstream.se
[Malhotra 01] Malhotra, Vivek. June 2001. Introduction to SMS. http://www105.ibm.com/developerworks

[Oreiljsw] http://www.oreilly.com/catalog/jswing/desc.html

[Preece] Preece.J., Human Computer Interaction, Addison-Wesley, 1994

[Preece99] Human Computer Interaction; Preece, Jenny; Addison-Wesley; 1999

[Press00] Pressman, R. S., Software Engineering, 'A Practitioner's Approach', European Adaptation, Fifth Edition, Adapted by: Ince, D. Page: 42

[Sharp] http://www.dhtml-zone.com/Nokia/Article/6969

[Shneid] Shneiderman, B., 1986, Designing the User Interface: Strategies for Effective Human-Computer Interaction, Addison-Wesley Publishing Company

[Simplewire] http://www.simplewire.com/

[SMS-Tut02] SMS Tutorial, http://www.visualgsm.com/wire_sms_index.htm

[Sommerville97] Sommerville, I. 'Software Engineering', Addison Wesley, USA. Pp: 138-144, 1997

[Sommv]Sommerville, I., *Software Engineering*, Addison Wesley, 1995

[Swing] http://java.sun.com/products/jfc/

[Sun] http://java.sun.com/j2se/

[Sun02] Sun Microsystems. (2002). *Comparing JavaServer Pages and Microsoft Active Server Pages Technologies.*

[Tull02] Tull, C. 2002. Introduction to SMS, http://www.devx.com/wireless/articles/sms/smsintro.asp

[WapFrm] http://www.wapforum.com/documents.asp OMA Multimedia Messaging Service version 1.1

[Yerkey01] Yerkey, N. (2001). *Active Server Pages for Database Web Access.* Library Hi Tech, 19:2 pp:133-142.

[3Gevo] http://www.tdap.co.uk/uk/archive/mobile

Appendix A: MMS_App.java

```java
/*
 * OriginatingApp.java
 *
 */

import java.io.*;
import java.awt.*;
import java.awt.event.*;
import javax.swing.*;
import javax.swing.filechooser.*;
import com.oxelis.swing.JFileChooserX;

public class MMS_App extends JFrame {
        private static  File flImageFileOne = null;
        private static  File flTextFileOne = null;
        private static  File flSoundFileOne = null;
        private static  File flImageFileTwo = null;
        private static  File flTextFileTwo = null;
        private static  File flSoundFileTwo = null;
        private static JTextField txtImageFile = new JTextField(9);
        private static JTextField txtTextFile = new JTextField(9);
        private static JTextField txtSoundFile = new JTextField(9);
        private static JTextField txtPhNum = new JTextField(15);

        static private final String newline = "\n";
        private static int slideCounter = 0;


    public MMS_App() {

        super("Multimedia Messaging Service");

        //Create the log first, because the action listeners
        //need to refer to it.
        final JTextArea log = new JTextArea(5,20);
        log.setMargin(new Insets(5,5,5,5));
        log.setEditable(false);
        JScrollPane logScrollPane = new JScrollPane(log);


        //Create a file chooser
        final JFileChooserX fc = new JFileChooserX();

        //Create the imageIcon to hold the image
        final ImageIcon ic = new ImageIcon("U:\\Multimedia Messaging
Application\\Image Files\\mms_main_new.jpg");

        //add the image to the label
        JLabel imageLabel = new JLabel(ic);
```

164

```java
//Create a panel to hold the textfields/labels/button
JPanel controlsPanel = new JPanel();
JLabel lbPhNum = new JLabel("        Enter Phone Number: ");
JLabel lbEmail = new JLabel("        Email Address (Optional): ");
JTextField txtEmail = new JTextField(9);
JButton btImage = new JButton("Add Image..");
JButton btText = new JButton("Add Text..");
JButton btSound = new JButton("Add Sound Clip..");
JButton btNewSlide = new JButton("New Slide..(2 slide max)");
JButton btSendButton = new JButton("Send Message");

//Set the layout for the panel
controlsPanel.setLayout(new GridLayout(6,2));

//Add the controls to the panel
controlsPanel.add(btImage);
controlsPanel.add(txtImageFile);
controlsPanel.add(btText);
controlsPanel.add(txtTextFile);
controlsPanel.add(btSound);
controlsPanel.add(txtSoundFile);
controlsPanel.add(btNewSlide);
controlsPanel.add(btSendButton);
controlsPanel.add(lbPhNum);
controlsPanel.add(txtPhNum);
controlsPanel.add(lbEmail);
controlsPanel.add(txtEmail);

btImage.addActionListener(new ActionListener() {
    public void actionPerformed(ActionEvent e) {
            fc.addChoosableFileFilter(new ImageFilter());
            fc.setAcceptAllFileFilterUsed(false);
            //Add the preview pane.
        fc.setAccessory(new ImagePreview(fc));

        int returnVal = fc.showDialog(MMS_App.this, "Attach");


        if (returnVal == JFileChooser.APPROVE_OPTION) {
                if(slideCounter == 0){
                        flImageFileOne  = fc.getSelectedFile();
                                txtImageFile.setText(flImageFileOne
.getName());
                                log.append(flImageFileOne.getPath()
+ newline);
                }
                else{
                        flImageFileTwo = fc.getSelectedFile();

        txtImageFile.setText(flImageFileTwo.getName());
                        log.append(flImageFileTwo.getPath() +
newline);
                }
```

```java
                    }
                }
            });

            btText.addActionListener(new ActionListener() {
                public void actionPerformed(ActionEvent e) {
                    fc.addChoosableFileFilter(new TextFilter());
                    fc.setAcceptAllFileFilterUsed(false);

                    int returnVal = fc.showDialog(MMS_App.this,
"Attach");

                    if (returnVal == JFileChooser.APPROVE_OPTION) {
                        if(slideCounter == 0){
                            flTextFileOne = fc.getSelectedFile();

        txtTextFile.setText(flTextFileOne.getName());
                            log.append(flTextFileOne.getPath() +
newline);
                        }
                        else{
                            flTextFileTwo = fc.getSelectedFile();

        txtTextFile.setText(flTextFileTwo.getName());
                            log.append(flTextFileTwo.getPath() +
newline);
                        }
                    }
                }
            });

            btSound.addActionListener(new ActionListener() {
                public void actionPerformed(ActionEvent e) {
                        fc.addChoosableFileFilter(new SoundFilter());
                    fc.setAcceptAllFileFilterUsed(false);

                    int returnVal = fc.showDialog(MMS_App.this,
"Attach");

                    if (returnVal ==
JFileChooser.APPROVE_OPTION) {
                    if(slideCounter == 0){
                            flSoundFileOne =
fc.getSelectedFile();

        txtSoundFile.setText(flSoundFileOne.getName());
                                log.append(flSoundFileOne.getPath()
+ newline);
                        }
                        else{
                            flSoundFileTwo =
fc.getSelectedFile();

        txtSoundFile.setText(flSoundFileTwo.getName());
```

```java
                            log.append(flSoundFileTwo.getPath()
+ newline);
                        }
                    }
        }
    });

    btNewSlide.addActionListener(new ActionListener() {
        public void actionPerformed(ActionEvent e) {
                if(slideCounter < 1)
                {

                        //check first that there is at least one file for
the first slide
                        if(flImageFileOne == null & flTextFileOne ==
null & flSoundFileOne == null)
                        {

        JOptionPane.showMessageDialog(null, "Error: Can't add new
slide as first slide is empty..", "alert", JOptionPane.ERROR_MESSAGE);

                        }
                        else{
                                //reset the text fields
                                    txtImageFile.setText("");
                                    txtTextFile.setText("");
                                    txtSoundFile.setText("");
                                //update the slide counter
to ensure that no file gets overwritten
                                    slideCounter++;
                        }
                }
                else
                        JOptionPane.showMessageDialog(null, "Error:
Maximum of two slides only permitted", "alert",
JOptionPane.ERROR_MESSAGE);
        }
    });

    btSendButton.addActionListener(new ActionListener() {
        public void actionPerformed(ActionEvent e) {
                log.append("fine");
                //int phoneNumber =
Integer.parseInt(txtPhNum.getText());
                if(txtPhNum.getText().equals(""))
                {
                        JOptionPane.showMessageDialog(null, "Please
enter mobile number.", "alert", JOptionPane.ERROR_MESSAGE);
                }
                else
                {
```

```java
                    //check to see what the message consists of, and then
send using correct parameters
                        if(slideCounter == 0)
                        {
                            if(flImageFileOne == null &
flTextFileOne == null & flSoundFileOne == null)
                            {

        JOptionPane.showMessageDialog(null, "Message Content
Empty, Please choose some..", "alert", JOptionPane.ERROR_MESSAGE);

                            }
                        else
                        {
                            OriginatingApp oa = new
OriginatingApp(flImageFileOne, flTextFileOne, flSoundFileOne);
                            log.append(newline +
"Message sent to " + txtPhNum.getText() + newline);
                                        //reset the text
fields

        txtImageFile.setText("");

        txtTextFile.setText("");

        txtSoundFile.setText("");

        txtPhNum.setText("");
                                        //set all the files to
equal null for the next message
                            flImageFileOne =
null;
                            flTextFileOne =
null;
                            flSoundFileOne =
null;
                                        //reset the slide
counter for the next message
                            slideCounter = 0;


                        }
                    }
                    else
                    {
                        OriginatingApp oa = new
OriginatingApp(flImageFileOne, flTextFileOne, flSoundFileOne,
flImageFileTwo, flTextFileTwo, flSoundFileTwo);

                        log.append(newline + "Message sent to " +
txtPhNum.getText() + newline);
                                //reset the text fields
                        txtImageFile.setText("");
                        txtTextFile.setText("");
```

```java
                              txtSoundFile.setText("");
                              txtPhNum.setText("");
                              //set all the files to equal null for the next
message
                              flImageFileOne = null;
                              flTextFileOne = null;
                              flSoundFileOne = null;
                              flImageFileTwo = null;
                              flTextFileTwo = null;
                              flSoundFileTwo = null;

                              //reset the slide counter for the next message

                slideCounter = 0;
                          }


                    }//if for testing the mobile number


          }
    });


    //Add the buttons and the log to the frame
    Container contentPane = getContentPane();
    contentPane.add(logScrollPane, BorderLayout.SOUTH);
    contentPane.add(imageLabel, BorderLayout.NORTH);
    contentPane.add(controlsPanel, BorderLayout.CENTER);
  }

  public static void main(String[] args)
{
                JFrame frame = new MMS_App();

                frame.addWindowListener(new WindowAdapter() {
                        public void windowClosing(WindowEvent e) {
                                System.exit(0);
                        }
                });

                frame.pack();
                frame.setVisible(true);
}//main
}//class
```

Appendix B: OriginatingApp.java

```java
/*
 * OriginatingApp.java
 */

import java.io.*;
import java.util.*;
import java.net.*;
import com.nokia.mms.*;

public class OriginatingApp {

public OriginatingApp(File imageFileOne, File textFileOne, File
soundFileOne) {
        MMMessage mm = new MMMessage();
        SetMessage(mm);
        AddContents(mm, imageFileOne, textFileOne, soundFileOne);
        MMEncoder encoder=new MMEncoder();
        encoder.setMessage(mm);

    try {
        encoder.encodeMessage();
      byte[] out = encoder.getMessage();

      MMSender sender = new MMSender();
      sender.setMMSCURL("http://127.0.0.1:8189");
      sender.addHeader("X-NOKIA-MMSC-Charging", "100");

      MMResponse mmResponse = sender.send(out);
      System.out.println("Message sent to " + sender.getMMSCURL());
      System.out.println("Response code: " +
mmResponse.getResponseCode() + " " +
mmResponse.getResponseMessage());

      Enumeration keys = mmResponse.getHeadersList();
      while (keys.hasMoreElements()){
        String key = (String) keys.nextElement();
        String value = (String) mmResponse.getHeaderValue(key);
        System.out.println(key + ": " + value);
      }

    } catch (Exception e) {
      System.out.println(e.getMessage());
    }
  }


public OriginatingApp(File imageFileOne, File textFileOne, File
soundFileOne, File imageFileTwo, File textFileTwo, File soundFileTwo) {
    MMMessage mm = new MMMessage();
    SetMessage(mm);
```

```java
    AddContents(mm, imageFileOne, textFileOne, soundFileOne,
imageFileTwo, textFileTwo, soundFileTwo);

    MMEncoder encoder=new MMEncoder();
    encoder.setMessage(mm);

    try {
      encoder.encodeMessage();
      byte[] out = encoder.getMessage();

      MMSender sender = new MMSender();
      sender.setMMSCURL("http://127.0.0.1:8189");
      sender.addHeader("X-NOKIA-MMSC-Charging", "100");

      MMResponse mmResponse = sender.send(out);
      System.out.println("Message sent to " + sender.getMMSCURL());
      System.out.println("Response code: " +
mmResponse.getResponseCode() + " " +
mmResponse.getResponseMessage());

      Enumeration keys = mmResponse.getHeadersList();
      while (keys.hasMoreElements()){
        String key = (String) keys.nextElement();
        String value = (String) mmResponse.getHeaderValue(key);
        System.out.println(key + ": " + value);
      }

    } catch (Exception e) {
      System.out.println(e.getMessage());
    }
  }

  private void SetMessage(MMMessage mm) {
    mm.setVersion(IMMConstants.MMS_VERSION_10);
    mm.setMessageType(IMMConstants.MESSAGE_TYPE_M_SEND_REQ);
    mm.setTransactionId("0000000066");
    mm.setDate(new Date(System.currentTimeMillis()));
    mm.setFrom("+358990000066/TYPE=PLMN");
    mm.addToAddress("+358990000005/TYPE=PLMN");
    mm.addToAddress("123.124.125.125/TYPE=IPv4");

mm.addToAddress("1234:5678:90AB:CDEF:FEDC:BA09:8765:4321/TYP
E=IPv6");
    mm.addToAddress("ro_to@hotmail.com");//"john.doe@nokia.com");
    mm.setDeliveryReport(true);
    mm.setReadReply(false);
    mm.setSenderVisibility(IMMConstants.SENDER_VISIBILITY_SHOW);
    mm.setSubject("This is a nice nice message!!");
    mm.setMessageClass(IMMConstants.MESSAGE_CLASS_PERSONAL);
    mm.setPriority(IMMConstants.PRIORITY_LOW);

mm.setContentType(IMMConstants.CT_APPLICATION_MULTIPART_MIXE
D);
```

```
//    In case of multipart related message and a smil presentation
available
//
mm.setContentType(IMMConstants.CT_APPLICATION_MULTIPART_RELA
TED);
//
mm.setMultipartRelatedType(IMMConstants.CT_APPLICATION_SMIL);
//    mm.setPresentationId("<A0>"); // where <A0> is the id of the
content containing the SMIL presentation
  }


private void AddContents(MMMessage mm, File imageFileOne, File
textFileOne, File soundFileOne) {
        /*Path where contents are stored*/
        String path = getPath();

        if(imageFileOne != null)
        {
                // Add slide1 image
                MMContent s1_image = new MMContent();
                byte[] b3 = readFile(imageFileOne.getAbsolutePath());
                s1_image.setContent(b3,0,b3.length);
                s1_image.setContentId("quick.gif");
                //set the image type based on the image selected by
the user
                if (imageFileOne.getName().endsWith(".gif"))

        s1_image.setType(IMMConstants.CT_IMAGE_GIF);
                                else

        s1_image.setType(IMMConstants.CT_IMAGE_JPEG);
                mm.addContent(s1_image);
        }

        if(textFileOne != null)
        {
                // Add slide1 text
                MMContent s1_text = new MMContent();
                                byte[] b2 =
readFile(textFileOne.getAbsolutePath());
                s1_text.setContent(b2,0,b2.length);
                s1_text.setContentId("HelloWorld.txt"); //If "<>" are
not used with this method, the result is Content-Location
                s1_text.setType(IMMConstants.CT_TEXT_PLAIN);
                mm.addContent(s1_text);
        }

        if(soundFileOne != null)
        {
                // Add slide1 audio
                MMContent s1_audio = new MMContent();
                byte[] b4 = readFile(soundFileOne.getAbsolutePath());
                s1_audio.setContent(b4,0,b4.length);
```

```java
                s1_audio.setContentId("<HelloWorld.amr>");
                s1_audio.setType("audio/amr"); //Note how to use
mime-types with no pre-defined constant!
                mm.addContent(s1_audio);
        }

    }//Add Contents



    private void AddContents(MMMessage mm, File imageFileOne, File
textFileOne, File soundFileOne, File imageFileTwo, File textFileTwo, File
soundFileTwo) {
        /*Path where contents are stored*/
        String path = getPath();

        if(imageFileOne != null)
                {
                    // Add slide1 image
                    MMContent s1_image = new MMContent();
                    byte[] b3 = readFile(imageFileOne.getAbsolutePath());
                    s1_image.setContent(b3,0,b3.length);
                    s1_image.setContentId("quick.gif");
                    //set the image type based on the image selected by
the user
                    if (imageFileOne.getName().endsWith(".gif"))

            s1_image.setType(IMMConstants.CT_IMAGE_GIF);
                                    else

            s1_image.setType(IMMConstants.CT_IMAGE_JPEG);
                        mm.addContent(s1_image);
                }

        if(textFileOne != null)
                {
                    // Add slide1 text
                    MMContent s1_text = new MMContent();
                                    byte[] b2 =
readFile(textFileOne.getAbsolutePath());
                        s1_text.setContent(b2,0,b2.length);
                        s1_text.setContentId("HelloWorld.txt"); //If "<>" are
not used with this method, the result is Content-Location
                        s1_text.setType(IMMConstants.CT_TEXT_PLAIN);
                        mm.addContent(s1_text);
                }

        if(soundFileOne != null)
                {
                    // Add slide1 audio
                    MMContent s1_audio = new MMContent();
                    byte[] b4 = readFile(soundFileOne.getAbsolutePath());
                    s1_audio.setContent(b4,0,b4.length);
                    s1_audio.setContentId("HelloWorld.amr");
```

173

```java
                s1_audio.setType("audio/amr"); //Note how to use
mime-types with no pre-defined constant!
                mm.addContent(s1_audio);
        }


    if(imageFileTwo != null)
        {
                // Add slide2 image
                MMContent s1_image = new MMContent();
                byte[] b5 = readFile(imageFileTwo.getAbsolutePath());
                s1_image.setContent(b5,0,b5.length);
                s1_image.setContentId("SSquick.gif");
                //set the image type based on the image selected by
the user
                if (imageFileTwo.getName().endsWith(".gif"))

        s1_image.setType(IMMConstants.CT_IMAGE_GIF);
                                else

        s1_image.setType(IMMConstants.CT_IMAGE_JPEG);
                mm.addContent(s1_image);
        }

    if(textFileTwo != null)
        {
                // Add slide2 text
                MMContent s1_text = new MMContent();
                                byte[] b6 =
readFile(textFileTwo.getAbsolutePath());
                s1_text.setContent(b6,0,b6.length);
                s1_text.setContentId("SSHelloWorld.txt"); //If "<>"
are not used with this method, the result is Content-Location
                s1_text.setType(IMMConstants.CT_TEXT_PLAIN);
                mm.addContent(s1_text);
        }

    if(soundFileTwo != null)
        {
                // Add slide2 audio
                MMContent s1_audio = new MMContent();
                byte[] b7 = readFile(soundFileTwo.getAbsolutePath());
                s1_audio.setContent(b7,0,b7.length);
                s1_audio.setContentId("<SSHelloWorld.amr>");
                s1_audio.setType("audio/amr"); //Note how to use
mime-types with no pre-defined constant!
                mm.addContent(s1_audio);
        }

    }//Add Contents


    private byte[] readFile(String filename) {
```

```java
    int fileSize=0;
    RandomAccessFile fileH=null;

    // Opens the file for reading.
    try {
      fileH = new RandomAccessFile(filename, "r");
      fileSize = (int) fileH.length();
    } catch (IOException ioErr) {
      System.err.println("Cannot find " + filename);
      System.err.println(ioErr);
      System.exit(200);
    }

    // allocates the buffer large enough to hold entire file
    byte[] buf = new byte[fileSize];

    // reads all bytes of file
    int i=0;
    try {
      while (true) {
        try {
          buf[i++] = fileH.readByte();
        } catch (EOFException e) {
         break;
        }
      }
    } catch (IOException ioErr) {
     System.out.println("ERROR in reading of file"+filename);
    }

    return buf;
  }

  private String getPath() {
    URL url = getClass().getResource(getClass().getName() + ".class");
    String classPath = url.getHost() + url.getFile();
    int pos = classPath.lastIndexOf("/");
    return classPath.substring(0, pos + 1);
  }


}
```

Appendix C: ImageFilter.java

```java
import java.io.File;
import javax.swing.*;
import javax.swing.filechooser.*;

/* ImageFilter.java is a 1.4 example used by FileChooserDemo2.java. */
public class ImageFilter extends FileFilter {

    //Accept all directories and all gif, jpeg, and jpg files.
    public boolean accept(File f) {
        if (f.isDirectory()) {
            return true;
        }

        String extension = Utils.getExtension(f);
        if (extension != null) {
            if (extension.equals(Utils.gif) ||
                extension.equals(Utils.jpeg) ||
                extension.equals(Utils.jpg)) {
                    return true;
            } else {
                return false;
            }
        }

        return false;
    }

    //The description of this filter
    public String getDescription() {
        return "Just Images";
    }
}
```

Appendix D: ImagePreview.java

```java
import javax.swing.*;
import java.beans.*;
import java.awt.*;
import java.io.File;

/* ImagePreview.java is a 1.4 example used by FileChooserDemo2.java.
*/
public class ImagePreview extends JComponent
                   implements PropertyChangeListener {
    ImageIcon thumbnail = null;
    File file = null;

    public ImagePreview(JFileChooser fc) {
        setPreferredSize(new Dimension(100, 50));
        fc.addPropertyChangeListener(this);
    }

    public void loadImage() {
        if (file == null) {
            thumbnail = null;
            return;
        }

        //Don't use createImageIcon (which is a wrapper for getResource)
        //because the image we're trying to load is probably not one
        //of this program's own resources.
        ImageIcon tmpIcon = new ImageIcon(file.getPath());
        if (tmpIcon != null) {
            if (tmpIcon.getIconWidth() > 90) {
                thumbnail = new ImageIcon(tmpIcon.getImage().
                              getScaledInstance(90, -1,
                                    Image.SCALE_DEFAULT));
            } else { //no need to miniaturize
                thumbnail = tmpIcon;
            }
        }
    }

    public void propertyChange(PropertyChangeEvent e) {
        boolean update = false;
        String prop = e.getPropertyName();

        //If the directory changed, don't show an image.
        if (JFileChooser.DIRECTORY_CHANGED_PROPERTY.equals(prop)) {
            file = null;
            update = true;
        //If a file became selected, find out which one.
        } else if
(JFileChooser.SELECTED_FILE_CHANGED_PROPERTY.equals(prop)) {
```

```java
                file = (File) e.getNewValue();
                update = true;
        }
        //Update the preview accordingly.
        if (update) {
            thumbnail = null;
            if (isShowing()) {
                loadImage();
                repaint();
            }
        }
    }
    public void paintComponent(Graphics g) {
        if (thumbnail == null) {
            loadImage();
        }
        if (thumbnail != null) {
            int x = getWidth()/2 - thumbnail.getIconWidth()/2;
            int y = getHeight()/2 - thumbnail.getIconHeight()/2;
            if (y < 0) {
                y = 0;
            }
            if (x < 5) {
                x = 5;
            }
            thumbnail.paintIcon(this, g, x, y);
        }
    }
}
```

Appendix E: SoundFilter.java

```java
import java.io.File;
import javax.swing.*;
import javax.swing.filechooser.*;

/* SoundFilter.java is a 1.4 example used by FileChooserDemo2.java. */
public class SoundFilter extends FileFilter {

    //Accept all directories and all amr and wav files.
    public boolean accept(File f) {
        if (f.isDirectory()) {
            return true;
        }

        String extension = Utils.getExtension(f);
        if (extension != null) {
            if (extension.equals(Utils.amr)||
                    extension.equals(Utils.wav)) {
                return true;
            } else {
                return false;
            }
        }

        return false;
    }

    //The description of this filter
    public String getDescription() {
        return "Just Sound Files";
    }
}
```

Appendix F: TextFilter.java

```java
import java.io.File;
import javax.swing.*;
import javax.swing.filechooser.*;

/* TextFilter.java is a 1.4 example used by FileChooserDemo2.java. */
public class TextFilter extends FileFilter {

    //Accept all directories and all txt files.
    public boolean accept(File f) {
        if (f.isDirectory()) {
            return true;
        }

        String extension = Utils.getExtension(f);
        if (extension != null) {
            if (extension.equals(Utils.txt)) {
                return true;
            } else {
                return false;
            }
        }

        return false;
    }

    //The description of this filter
    public String getDescription() {
        return "Just Text Files";
    }
}
```

Appendix G: Utils.java

```java
import java.io.File;
import javax.swing.ImageIcon;

/* Utils.java is a 1.4 example used by FileChooserDemo2.java. */
public class Utils {
    public final static String jpeg = "jpeg";
    public final static String jpg = "jpg";
    public final static String gif = "gif";
    public final static String txt = "txt";
    public final static String amr = "amr";
    public final static String wav = "wav";


    /*
     * Get the extension of a file.
     */
    public static String getExtension(File f) {
        String ext = null;
        String s = f.getName();
        int i = s.lastIndexOf('.');

        if (i > 0 &&  i < s.length() - 1) {
            ext = s.substring(i+1).toLowerCase();
        }
        return ext;
    }

    /** Returns an ImageIcon, or null if the path was invalid. */
    protected static ImageIcon createImageIcon(String path) {
        java.net.URL imgURL = Utils.class.getResource(path);
        if (imgURL != null) {
            return new ImageIcon(imgURL);
        } else {
            System.err.println("Couldn't find file: " + path);
            return null;
        }
    }

}
```

Appendix H: Simplewire Network Coverage

The following is a complete list of worldwide network providers supported by the Simplewire wireless messaging network and the amount of credits charged per message by each [Simplewire] :

Country	Network Provider	Credits Per Message
Albania Albanian	Mobile Communications	2
Algeria	AMN (MPTT)	2
Andorra	STA	2
Argentina	Nextel	2
Australia	Optus	2
Australia	Telstra Corporation Limited	2
Australia	Vodafone Pty Ltd.	2
Austria	Connect Austria	2
Austria	max.mobil Telekomm GmbH	2
Austria	Telering	2
Azerbaijan	Azercell Telekom	2
Azerbaijan	J.V. Bakcell	2
Bahrain	Batelco	2
Bangladesh	GrameenPhone Ltd.	2
Belarus	JV Mobile Digital Comms	2
Belgium	Belgacom	3
Belgium	Mobistar	3
Bosnia/Herzegovina	Eronet	2
Bosnia/Herzegovina	Mobilna Srpske	2
Bosnia/Herzegovina	PTT BIH	2
Botswana	Mascom Wireless (Pty) Ltd.	2
Botswana	Vista Cellular	2
Brazil	Nextel	2
Brunei	Darussalam DST Comms	2
Bulgaria	MobilTEL AD	2
Cambodia	CamGSM Company Ltd	2
Cambodia	CASACOM	2
Cameroon	SCM	2
Canada	Bell Mobility	1
Canada	Clearnet	1
Canada	Fido	1
Canada	Microcell Telecomms Inc.	2
Canada	Pagemart Canada	1
Canada	Rogers AT&T Paging	1
Canada	Rogers AT&T Wireless	1

Canada	Sasktel Paging	1
Canada	Sasktel PCS	1
Canada	Shaw Paging	1
Canada	Telus Mobility	1
Cape Verde	Cape Verde Telecom	2
Chile	Entel Telefonia Movil S.A	2
China	China Unicom	2
China	MPT, China Telecom	2
CÔte d'Ivoire	Loteny Telecom	2
CÔte d'Ivoire	Société Ivoiri. Mobiles (SIM)	2
Croatia	Croatian Telecom	2
Croatia	vipnet GSM d.o.o.	2
Cyprus	Cyprus Telecom Authority	2
Czech Republic	Cesky Mobil a.s.	2
Czech Republic	Eurotel Praha	2
Czech Republic	Radiomobil, Praha	2
Denmark	Dansk Mobil Telefon	2
Denmark	Mobilix	2
Denmark	Sonofon	2
Denmark	TeleDanmark Mobil	2
Denmark	Telia A/S, Denmark	2
Dominican Republic	AACR	1
Dominican Republic	Tricom	1
Egypt	ECMS MoBiNil	2
Egypt	MisrFone Telecomms Co., SAE	2
Equatorial Guinea	Getesa	2
Estonia	AS EMT	2
Estonia	AS Ritabell	2
Estonia	Radiolinja Eesti AS	2
Faroe Islands	Faroese Telecom	2
Fiji	Vodafone Fiji Ltd.	2
Finland	Åland Mobiltelefon AB	2
Finland	Oy Radiolinja Ab	2
Finland	Sonera Corporation	2
Finland	Suomen 2G	2
France	Bouygues	2
France	France Caraibe Mobiles	2
France	France Telecom	2
France	SFR	2
Georgia	Geocell Ltd.	2
Georgia	Magticom Ltd.	2
Germany	D2 Vodafone	2
Germany	DeTeMobil	2
Germany	E Plus	2
Germany	VIAG Interkom	3
Ghana	ScanCom Ltd.	2
Gibraltar	Gibtel	2
Greece	Cellular Operating System Mobile Tel.	2

Greece	Panafon	2
Greece	STET Hellas	2
Greenland	TELE Greenland A/S	2
Holy (Vatican City)	Telecom Italia/Omnitel/Wind	2
Hong Kong	HKTCSL	2
Hong Kong	Hutchison	2
Hong Kong	Mandarin Communications Ltd.	2
Hong Kong	New World PCS, Ltd.	2
Hong Kong	Peoples Telephone Ltd.	2
Hong Kong	Smartone 900/1800/1900	2
Hungary	Pannon GSM	2
Hungary	V.R.A.M. Telecomms Company	2
Hungary	Westel 900 GSM	2
Iceland	Iceland Telecom Ltd.	2
Iceland	TAL Ltd.	2
India	Bharti Cellular Ltd.	2
India	Bharti Mobile Ltd.	2
India	Birla AT&T Gujarat	2
India	Birla AT&T Maharashtra/Goa	2
India	BPL Cellular Limited	2
India	BPL Mobile Comms Ltd.	2
India	Escotel	2
India	Fascel Limited	2
India	Hexacom India Ltd.	2
India	Hutchison Max Telecom Pvt	2
India	RPG Cellular Services	2
India	Skycell Communications Ltd.	2
India	Spice Communications Ltd.	2
India	SpiceCell Ltd.	2
India	Sterling Cellular Ltd.	2
India	TATA Communications Ltd.	2
India	Usha Martin Telekom Ltd.	2
Indonesia	PT Excelcomindo Pratama	2
Indonesia	PT Telekomunikasi Palapa,	2
Indonesia	PT.Satelit Palapa Indonesia	2
Ireland	Eircell	2
Ireland	Esat Digifone	2
Israel	Palestine Cellular Telecom Ltd.	2
Israel	Partner Comms Company Ltd	2
Italy	Blu	3
Italy	Omnitel Pronto Italia	3
Italy	Telecom Italia Mobile	3
Italy	Wind Telecomunicazioni SpA	3
Jordan	Jordan Mobile Telephone	2
Jordan	MobileCom	2
Kazakstan	GSM Kazakhstan, K'Cell	2
Kazakstan	KaR-Tel LLC	2
Kenya	ncell	2

Kuwait	Mobile Telecom. Co. (K.S.C.)	2
Kuwait	Wataniya Telecom	2
Kyrgyzstan	Bitel Ltd.	2
Latvia	Baltcom GSM	2
Latvia	Latvian Mobile Telephone ltd.	2
Lebanon	FTML	2
Lebanon	LibanCell	2
Liechtenstein	mobilkom Liechstenstein	2
Liechtenstein	Tele2 AG, Liechtenstein	2
Liechtenstein	Telecom FL	2
Lithuania	Omnitel Lithuania	2
Lithuania	UAB Bité GSM, Vilnius	2
Luxembourg	P&T Luxembourg	2
Luxembourg	Tango SA	2
Macau	C.T.M Macau	2
Macedonia	Post and Telecom Makedonija	2
Madagascar	Madacom SA	2
Malaysia	Celcom SDN BHD	2
Malaysia	DiGi Telecomms Sdn Bhd	2
Malaysia	Maxis Telecomm Sdn Bhd	2
Malaysia	Time Wireless (former Sapura)	2
Malaysia	TMTouch	2
Maldives	Dhiraagu	2
Malta	go mobile	2
Malta	Vodafone Malta Limited	2
Mauritius	Cellplus Mobile Telecom. Ltd.	2
Mauritius	Emtel	2
Mexico	Nextel	2
Moldova, Republic of	Moldcell	2
Moldova, Republic of	VoxTel SA	2
Monaco	France Telecm/SFR/Bouygues	2
Morocco	Itissalat Al Maghrib SA	2
Morocco	Meditelecom	2
Mozambique	Telecoms de Mocambique	2
Namibia	Mobile Telecommunications	2
Netherlands	Ben Nederland BV	2
Netherlands	Dutchtone NV	2
Netherlands	KPN Telecom BV	2
Netherlands	Libertel BV	2
Netherlands	Telfort Holding BV	2
New Zealand	Vodafone New Zealand	2
Norway	Netcom GSM AS	2
Oman	GTO, Ministry of PTT	2
Pakistan	Pakistan Mobile Comms Ltd.	2
Peru	Nextel	2
Philippines	Globe Telecom GMCR Inc.	2
Philippines	Isla Communications Co., Inc.	2
Philippines	Nextel	2

Philippines	Smart Communications Inc.	2
Poland	Polkomtel S.A., Warsaw	2
Poland	Polska Telefonia Cyfrowa - PTC	2
Poland	PTK Centertel	2
Portugal	Main Road Telecoms S.A.	2
Portugal	Telecel	2
Portugal	Telecomunicações Móveis Nac.	2
Qatar	Qatar Telecomms Corp.	2
RÉunion	Sté Ré du Radiotéléphone	2
Romania	Cosmorom	2
Romania	MobiFon SA	2
Romania	MobilRom	2
Russian Federation	Emark RMS	2
Russian Federation	Extel Mobile Com. System	2
Russian Federation	Cellular Systems-900	2
Russian Federation	JSC Dontelecom	2
Russian Federation	KB Impuls	2
Russian Federation	Kuban-GSM	2
Russian Federation	Mobile Telesystems	2
Russian Federation	Nizhegorodskaya Cellular	2
Russian Federation	North-West GSM	2
Russian Federation	NTC New Telephone Company	2
Russian Federation	Siberian Cellular Systems	2
Russian Federation	StavTeleSot	2
Russian Federation	Uraltel	2
Russian Federation	ZAO SMARTS	2
San Marino	Telecom Italia/Omnitel/Wind	2
Saudi Arabia	Electronic Appls Establishment	2
Saudi Arabia	Saudi Telecom Company	2
Senegal	Sentel GSM S.A.	2
Senegal	Sonatel S.A.	2
Seychelles	Cable and Wireless Ltd.	2
Seychelles	Telecom Seychelles limited	2
Singapore	MobileOne Pte Ltd, Singapore	2
Singapore	Singapore Telecom Mobile	2
Singapore	Singapore Telecom Mobile	2
Singapore	StarHub	2
Slovakia	EuroTel Bratislava	2
Slovakia	Globtel (SK)	2
Slovenia	MobiTel d.d., Slovenia	2
Slovenia	SI.MOBIL D.D.	2
South Africa	Mobile Telephone Networks	2
South Africa	Vodacom Pty Ltd.	2
Spain	Airtel	2
Sri Lanka	MTN Networks (PVT)	2
Sudan	Sudanese Mobile Co. Ltd.	2
Sweden	Comviq GSM AB	2
Sweden	Europolitan AB	2

Sweden	Telia Mobitel	2
Switzerland	diAx	2
Switzerland	Orange	2
Switzerland	Swisscom	2
Taiwan	Chunghwa Telecom (LDTA)	2
Taiwan	Far Eas Tone Telecomms Co.	2
Taiwan	KG Telecom Co.	2
Taiwan	Mobitai Communications Corp.	2
Taiwan	Taiwan Cellular Corp.	2
Taiwan,	TransAsia Telecommunications	2
Tanzania	TRI Telecoms (T) Ltd.	2
Thailand	Advanced Info. Service PLC	2
Thailand	Total Access Commun PCL.	2
Togo	Togo Cellulaire	2
Tunisia	Tunisie Telecom, Tunicell	2
Turkey	Telsim	2
Turkey	Turkcell	2
Turkmenistan	BCTI	2
Uganda	CelTel Cellular	2
Uganda	MTN Uganda Ltd.	2
Ukraine	Golden Telecom Bancomsvyaz	2
Ukraine	Kyivstar GSM JSC	2
Ukraine	Ukrainian Mobile Communs	2
Ukraine	Ukrainian Radio Systems	2
United Arab Emirates	Etisalat	2
United Kingdom	BT Cellnet	2
United Kingdom	Guernsey Telecoms	2
United Kingdom	Jersey Telecoms	2
United Kingdom	Manx Telecom	2
United Kingdom	One 2 One	2
United Kingdom	Orange PCS Ltd.	2
United Kingdom	Virgin Mobile	2
United Kingdom	Vodafone Ltd.	2
United States	Aerial	2
United States	Airtouch	1
United States	Alltel	1
United States	Alltel - GTE	1
United States	Alltel - Southwest	1
United States	Ameritech Paging	1
United States	Aquis Communications	1
United States	Arch Communications	1
United States	AT&T Wireless	1
United States	Cincinnati Bell	1
United States	Cingular - Ameritech	1
United States	Cingular - Bell South IPS	1
United States	Cingular - Bellsouth Mobility	1
United States	Cingular - Cellular One	1
United States	Cingular - Houston Cellular	1

United States	Cingular - Nevada Bell	1
United States	Cingular - Pacific Bell	1
United States	Cingular - Southwestern Bell	1
United States	Edge Wireless	1
United States	MCI	1
United States	Metrocall	1
United States	Midwest Wireless	1
United States	Nextel	1
United States	NPI Wireless	1
United States	OmniPoint	1
United States	Pagemart	1
United States	PageNet	1
United States	Powertel	2
United States	PrimeCo	1
United States	Skytel	1
United States	Smartbeep	1
United States	Sprint PCS	1
United States	TSR Wireless	1
United States	US Cellular	1
United States	US West	1
United States	Verizon	1
United States	Voicestream	1
United States	Weblink Wireless	1
United States	Weblink Wireless 2-Way	1
Uzbekistan	Coscom	2
Venezuela	Corporacion Digitel C.A.	2
Vietnam	Vietnam Mobile Telecom.	2
Vietnam	VinaPhone (GPC)	2
Western Sahara	Itissalat Al Maghrib SA	2
Yugoslavia	Mobile Telecomms Srbija	2
Yugoslavia	Monaco Telecom	2
Yugoslavia	Promonte	2
Yugoslavia	Telecom Srbija	2
Yugoslavia	Telekom Crne Gore	2
Zimbabwe	Econet Wireless	2
Zimbabwe	Posts and Telecomms Corp.	2
Zimbabwe	Telecel Zimbabwe	2

Appendix J: SMS Application Java Source Code

The following is a complete listing of Java classes used in the implementation of the SMS Messenger application.

1. Interface.java
2. FinalTest.java
3. AddContact.java
4. TextForm.java
5. DisplayContacts.java
6. Contact.java
7. Sorts.java
8. DisplayTextForm
9. AddGroup.java
10. DisplayTheGroups.java
11. Group.java
12. DisplayGroups.java
13. GatherGroupContacts.java
14. ShowGroupContacts.java
15. Implementation.java
16. Id_Password.java

The above list is in the same order as they appear in the book text. The entire SMS Messenger application excluding the classes provided by Simplewire consists of approximately 2,000 lines of code. The classes are as follows.

1. Interface.java

```java
import java.awt.*;
import java.awt.event.*;
import java.util.StringTokenizer;
import javax.swing.*;
import com.simplewire.sms.*;//obtained from www.simplewire.com
import javax.swing.JOptionPane;
import java.io.*;

public class Interface extends JPanel {
    private GridBagLayout layout;
    private GridBagConstraints constraints;
        private JPanel panel;
        private JTextArea messagefield = new JTextArea( 7, 15 );
    public JTextField numberfield = new JTextField( 15 );
        public JButton send;
    private JTextField fromfield = new JTextField( 15 );
    private JTextField cnumberfield = new JTextField( 15);
        public JTextArea feedback = new JTextArea( 1, 27 );

    // set up GUI
    public Interface()
    {
        Object newSettings[] = {"Button.background", new Color(208, 224,
240),
                                    "Button.foreground", new Color(0, 0,
144),    "Panel.background",
                                    new Color(255, 255, 255),
        "CheckBox.background", new Color(255,
                                    255, 255),
        "CheckBox.foreground", new Color(0, 0, 144),
                                    "Label.foreground", new
Color(0, 0, 144), "Label.font",
                                    new Font("SansSerif",
Font.PLAIN, 14)
                            };
                            UIDefaults defaults =
UIManager.getDefaults();
                            defaults.putDefaults(newSettings);

                        setLayout( new BorderLayout() );

        // instantiate gridbag constraints
        constraints = new GridBagConstraints();
        constraints.insets = new Insets( 0, 5, 5, 10 );

        // create GUI components
                        JLabel title, mnumber, from, cnumber, message,
space, space2;
                        title = new JLabel("SMS Messenger");
                        title.setFont(new Font( "Serif", Font.BOLD, 20));
                        mnumber = new JLabel(" Mobile No.");
                        from = new JLabel(" From");
```

```java
                    cnumber = new JLabel(" Callback No.");
                    message = new JLabel(" Message");
                    space = new JLabel("      ");
                    space2 = new JLabel("      ");
                    messagefield.setLineWrap(true);
                    messagefield.setWrapStyleWord(true);

        messagefield.setBorder(BorderFactory.createLineBorder(Color.g
ray));
                    feedback.setLineWrap(true);
                    feedback.setWrapStyleWord(true);
                    feedback.setEditable(false);
                    feedback.setForeground(new Color(0, 0, 144));

                    send = new JButton( "Send" );
                    send.addActionListener(new ActionListener() {

        public void actionPerformed(ActionEvent actionevent)
    {

        send();

    }

});

    JButton clear = new JButton( "Clear" );
    clear.addActionListener(new ActionListener() {

        public void actionPerformed(ActionEvent actionevent)
    {
        numberfield.setText("");
        fromfield.setText("");
        cnumberfield.setText("");
        messagefield.setText("");
    }

});


    JButton close = new JButton( "Close" );
    close.addActionListener(new ActionListener() {

        public void actionPerformed(ActionEvent actionevent)
    {
        System.exit(0);
    }

});

                    layout = new GridBagLayout();
                    panel = new JPanel();
                    panel.setLayout(layout);
```

```
                constraints.weightx = 1;
                        constraints.weighty = 1;
                constraints.gridwidth = GridBagConstraints.REMAINDER;
                addComponent( title );

                        constraints.anchor = GridBagConstraints.WEST;
                        constraints.gridwidth = 1;
                        addComponent( mnumber );

                        constraints.anchor = GridBagConstraints.CENTER;
                        constraints.gridwidth =
        GridBagConstraints.REMAINDER;
                    addComponent( numberfield );

                        constraints.anchor = GridBagConstraints.WEST;
                        constraints.gridwidth = 1;
                addComponent( from );

                        constraints.anchor = GridBagConstraints.CENTER;
                        constraints.gridwidth =
        GridBagConstraints.REMAINDER;
                    addComponent( fromfield );

                        constraints.anchor = GridBagConstraints.WEST;
                        constraints.gridwidth = 1;
                addComponent( cnumber );

                        constraints.anchor = GridBagConstraints.CENTER;
                        constraints.gridwidth =
        GridBagConstraints.REMAINDER;
                    addComponent( cnumberfield );

                        constraints.anchor = GridBagConstraints.WEST;
                        constraints.gridwidth = 1;
                addComponent( message );

                        constraints.anchor = GridBagConstraints.CENTER;
                        constraints.gridwidth =
        GridBagConstraints.REMAINDER;
                    addComponent( messagefield );

                        constraints.anchor = GridBagConstraints.WEST;
                        constraints.gridwidth = 1;
                addComponent( space );

                        constraints.anchor = GridBagConstraints.EAST;
                        constraints.gridwidth = 1;
                addComponent( send );

                        constraints.anchor = GridBagConstraints.WEST;
                        constraints.gridwidth =
        GridBagConstraints.REMAINDER;
                    addComponent( clear );
```

```java
        constraints.gridwidth = 1;
    addComponent( space2 );

        constraints.anchor = GridBagConstraints.CENTER;
        constraints.gridwidth =
GridBagConstraints.REMAINDER;
        addComponent( close );

        constraints.gridwidth =
GridBagConstraints.REMAINDER;
        addComponent( feedback );

        add(panel, BorderLayout.NORTH);

}//end constructor


//send message
private void send()
    {

            int countUnsuccessfull = 0;

            String feedbackText = "";

            // Create a StringTokenizer with a "," as a
delimiter
        StringTokenizer tokenizer = new StringTokenizer(
numberfield.getText(),

                        "," );
            while (tokenizer.hasMoreTokens()) {
                String aNumber =
tokenizer.nextToken();

                //obtained from Simplewires
software development kit
                SMS sms = new SMS();

                try {

                        // Create the buffered
reader for reading the file
                        BufferedReader inFile = new
BufferedReader(new FileReader(

        "subscriber.ini" ));

                        // Get the first line of the
file
                    String line = inFile.readLine();

                        // Subscriber Settings
```

193

```java
        sms.setSubscriberID(line);//Set the Subscriber ID property to
your
//Simplewire Developer ID
// Get the second line of the file

        line = inFile.readLine();
        sms.setSubscriberPassword(line);//got from developer settings
                        } // end try
                catch (IOException e) {
                System.err.println("Error: " + e);
                        }
                                // Message Settings
                                sms.setMsgPin(aNumber);//also
referred to as the mobile phone number

        sms.setMsgFrom(fromfield.getText());
        sms.setMsgCallback(cnumberfield.getText());
        sms.setMsgText(messagefield.getText());
        System.out.println("Sending message to " + aNumber);

// Send Message
//obtained from Simplewires software development kit
                                sms.msgSend();

                                // Check For Error
                                //obtained from Simplewires
software development kit –

                                //modified (feedback....)
                                if(sms.isSuccess())
                                {

        System.out.println("Message was sent to " + aNumber + "!");
                                feedback.setText("Message
was sent");
                                }
                                else        //obtained from Simplewires
software development kit –

                                //modified (feedback....etc)
                                {

                                        if(countUnsuccessfull<1)
                                        {
                                                feedbackText +=
"Message was not sent to:";
                                        }

                                        countUnsuccessfull++;


        System.out.println("Message was not sent to " + aNumber +
"!");
                                        System.out.println("Error
Code: " + sms.getErrorCode());
```

```java
                                        System.out.println("Error
Description: " + sms.getErrorDesc());
                                        System.out.println("Error
Resolution: " + sms.getErrorResolution()

        + "\n");
                                        feedbackText += "\n" +
aNumber + " " + sms.getErrorDesc() + " " +
                sms.getErrorResolution();
                        }
                }//end while
                if(countUnsuccessfull == 0)
            {
                        if(numberfield.getText() == null ||
numberfield.getText().equals(""))
feedback.setText("Please enter a number into the Mobile No.
                                field");
            }
                else
            {
        feedback.setText("Message was not sent");

        JOptionPane.showMessageDialog(null, feedbackText,
                "", JOptionPane.ERROR_MESSAGE );
            }
        }// end method send()
    // method to set constraints on
    private void addComponent( Component component )
    {
        layout.setConstraints( component, constraints );
        panel.add( component );
    }

} // end class
```

2. FinalTest.java

```java
//This class brings all the classes together
import java.awt.*;
import java.awt.event.*;
import javax.swing.*;
import javax.swing.event.*;
import java.io.*;
import javax.swing.JOptionPane;

public class FinalTest extends JFrame {
        private Interface messagePanel;
        private DisplayContacts contacts;
        private DisplayTheGroups groups;
        private GatherGroupContacts contacts2;
        private JCheckBox checkAll, checkAllGroup;
        private JButton addButton, addButtonGroup, addContactButton,
                addGroupContactButton, showAllButtonGroup, deleteButton,
                deleteButtonGroup;

        // set up GUI
        public FinalTest()
        {
                super( "SMS Text Messaging" );

                setBackground(new Color(255, 255, 255));

                Object newSettings[] = {"Button.background", new Color(208, 224, 240),
                                "Button.foreground", new Color(0, 0, 144),
                                "Panel.background", new Color(255, 255, 255),
                                "CheckBox.font", new Font("SansSerif", Font.PLAIN, 12),
                                "CheckBox.background", new Color(255, 255, 255),
                                "CheckBox.foreground", new Color(0, 0, 144),
                                "Label.foreground", new Color(0, 0, 144), "Label.font",
                                new Font("SansSerif", Font.PLAIN, 12),
                                "OptionPane.background", new Color(255, 255, 255),
                                "OptionPane.messageForeground", new Color(0, 0, 144),
                                "ScrollBar.background", new Color(255, 255, 255)
                        };
                UIDefaults defaults = UIManager.getDefaults();
                defaults.putDefaults(newSettings);
```

```
messagePanel = new Interface ();
        String contactsFile = "contacts";
        contacts = new DisplayContacts (contactsFile);
        groups = new DisplayTheGroups ();

        JPanel buttonPanel = new JPanel();
        FlowLayout buttonLayout = new FlowLayout();
        buttonPanel.setLayout(buttonLayout);
        buttonLayout.setAlignment( FlowLayout.LEFT );

        JPanel contactsPanel = new JPanel();
        contactsPanel.setLayout(new BorderLayout ());

        //get content pane and set its layout
    Container container = getContentPane();

        addButton = new JButton("<< Add");
        addButton.addActionListener(new ActionListener() {

    public void actionPerformed(ActionEvent actionevent)
    {
    String numbers = "";
    numbers += messagePanel.numberfield.getText();
    for(int i=0; i<contacts.contacts.length; i++) {

    if(contacts.form.checkBox[i].isSelected()) {
                                        numbers +=
contacts.contacts[i].getMobileNumComma();
                                }//end if
        } //end for

    messagePanel.numberfield.setText(numbers);
    }

        });

        addButtonGroup = new JButton("<< Add");
        addButtonGroup.setVisible(false);
        addButtonGroup.addActionListener(new
ActionListener() {

    public void actionPerformed(ActionEvent actionevent)
    {
    String numbers = "";
    numbers += messagePanel.numberfield.getText();
    for(int i=0; i<groups.groups.length; i++) {

    if(groups.form.checkBox[i].isSelected()) {
                                        contacts2 = new
GatherGroupContacts(groups.groups[i].getName());

    System.out.println(groups.groups[i].getName());
```

```java
                                                       for(int x=0;
x<contacts2.contacts.length; x++) {

        System.out.println(contacts2.contacts[x].toString());
                                               numbers
+= contacts2.contacts[x].getMobileNumComma();
                                      } // end inner for
                             }//end if
    } //end outer for

    messagePanel.numberfield.setText(numbers);
}

    });

            addContactButton = new JButton("Add Contact");
            addContactButton.addActionListener(new
ActionListener() {

    public void actionPerformed(ActionEvent actionevent)
{
    String name = "contacts";
    AddContact addcontact = new AddContact(name);


    addcontact.setDefaultCloseOperation(JFrame.HIDE_ON_CLOSE
);

    setVisible( false );

}

    });

            addGroupContactButton = new JButton("Add Group");
            addGroupContactButton.setVisible(false);
            addGroupContactButton.addActionListener(new
ActionListener() {

    public void actionPerformed(ActionEvent actionevent)
{
    AddGroup addgroup = new AddGroup();


    addgroup.setDefaultCloseOperation(JFrame.HIDE_ON_CLOSE );

    setVisible( false );

}

    });

            deleteButton = new JButton("Delete");
            deleteButton.addActionListener(new ActionListener() {
```

```java
        public void actionPerformed(ActionEvent actionevent)
    {
        try {
                FileWriter writer = new FileWriter( "contacts.txt",
false);
                                PrintWriter pw = new
PrintWriter( writer, true);

                for(int i=0; i<contacts.contacts.length; i++) {

        if(contacts.form.checkBox[i].isSelected()==false) {
                                pw.println(
contacts.contacts[i].getLastName() + "|" +

                                contacts.contacts[i].getFirstName()
+ "|"

                + contacts.contacts[i].getMobileNumPlain() + "|" +

                contacts.contacts[i].getEmail());
                        }//end if
                } //end for
                pw.flush();
                pw.close();
        } catch (IOException exception) {
                System.out.println("Error adding contact");
                        exception.printStackTrace();
                        } //end catch

        setVisible( false );

        FinalTest finaltest = new FinalTest();


        finaltest.setDefaultCloseOperation(JFrame.EXIT_ON_CLOSE );
    }

        });

                showAllButtonGroup = new JButton("Show All");
                showAllButtonGroup.setVisible(false);
                showAllButtonGroup.addActionListener(new
ActionListener() {

        public void actionPerformed(ActionEvent actionevent)
    {
        int count = 0;
        for(int i=0; i<groups.groups.length; i++) {
                if(groups.form.checkBox[i].isSelected()) {
                        count++;
                }//end if
        }//end for
```

```java
if(count>1) {
        JOptionPane.showMessageDialog(null, "Only one set of
Group contacts

        can be shown at once",    "", JOptionPane.WARNING_MESSAGE
);
        }
        else if(count==0) {
                JOptionPane.showMessageDialog(null, "A Group must
be selected from

        the list", "", JOptionPane.WARNING_MESSAGE );
        }

        else {
                for(int i=0; i<groups.groups.length; i++) {
                        if(groups.form.checkBox[i].isSelected()) {
                                ShowGroupContacts showAll =
                                new
ShowGroupContacts(groups.groups[i].getName());

        showAll.setDefaultCloseOperation(JFrame.EXIT_ON_CLOSE );
                        }//end if
                }//end for
        }//end else
    }
        });
                deleteButtonGroup = new JButton("Delete");
                deleteButtonGroup.setVisible(false);
                deleteButtonGroup.addActionListener(new
ActionListener() {
        public void actionPerformed(ActionEvent actionevent)
    {
        try {
                FileWriter writer = new FileWriter( "groups.txt", false);
                                PrintWriter pw = new
PrintWriter( writer, true);
                for(int i=0; i<groups.groups.length; i++) {
                        if(groups.form.checkBox[i].isSelected()) {
                                String groupfilename =
groups.groups[i].getName() + ".txt";
                                boolean success = (new
File(groupfilename)).delete();
                                        if (!success)
                                        System.out.println("Failed
to delete group file");
                        }//end outer if
                        else
if(groups.form.checkBox[i].isSelected()==false) {
                                pw.println(
groups.groups[i].getName() );
                        }//end else if
                } //end for
                pw.flush();
```

```java
                    pw.close();
            } catch (IOException exception) {
                    System.out.println("Error adding contact");
                            exception.printStackTrace();
                            } //end catch

        setVisible( false );
        FinalTest finaltest = new FinalTest();
        finaltest.setDefaultCloseOperation(JFrame.EXIT_ON_CLOSE );
    }
        });
                    checkAll = new JCheckBox ("Check All");
                    checkAll.addActionListener(new ActionListener() {
        public void actionPerformed(ActionEvent actionevent)
    {

        for(int i=0; i<contacts.contacts.length; i++) {
                if(checkAll.isSelected())
                            contacts.form.checkBox[i].setSelected(true);
                else
        contacts.form.checkBox[i].setSelected(false);
        }
    }
        });
                    checkAllGroup = new JCheckBox ("Check All");
                    checkAllGroup.setVisible(false);
                    checkAllGroup.addActionListener(new ActionListener()
{

        public void actionPerformed(ActionEvent actionevent)
    {
        for(int i=0; i<groups.groups.length; i++) {
                if(checkAllGroup.isSelected())
                            groups.form.checkBox[i].setSelected(true);
                else
                            groups.form.checkBox[i].setSelected(false);
        }
    }
        });
                    JLabel contactsTitle = new JLabel("Contacts");
        contactsTitle.setFont(new Font( "Serif", Font.BOLD, 20));

                    buttonPanel.add(checkAll);
                    buttonPanel.add(checkAllGroup);
                    buttonPanel.add(addButton);
                    buttonPanel.add(addButtonGroup);
                    buttonPanel.add(addContactButton);
                    buttonPanel.add(addGroupContactButton);
                    buttonPanel.add(showAllButtonGroup);
                    buttonPanel.add(deleteButton);
                    buttonPanel.add(deleteButtonGroup);

                    // Specify on which edge the tabs should appear
    int location = JTabbedPane.TOP; // or BOTTOM, LEFT, RIGHT

                    // Create the tabbed pane
```

201

```java
                        UIManager.put("TabbedPane.selected", new
        Color(208, 224, 240));
            JTabbedPane pane = new JTabbedPane();
                        pane.setBackground(new Color(255, 255, 255));
                        pane.setForeground(new Color(0, 0, 144));

                        // Add tabs
            pane.addTab("Individuals", contacts);
            pane.addTab("Groups", groups );

                        // Ref: modified code accessed from:
                        // http://javaalmanac.com/egs/javax.swing/pkg.html
                        ChangeListener changeListener = new
        ChangeListener() {
            public void stateChanged(ChangeEvent changeEvent) {
                JTabbedPane sourceTabbedPane =
        (JTabbedPane)changeEvent.getSource();
                int index = sourceTabbedPane.getSelectedIndex();
                if(index == 0)
                        {
                checkAll.setVisible(true);
                        addButton.setVisible(true);
                        addContactButton.setVisible(true);
                        deleteButton.setVisible(true);
                        checkAllGroup.setVisible(false);
                        addButtonGroup.setVisible(false);
                        addGroupContactButton.setVisible(false);
                        showAllButtonGroup.setVisible(false);
                        deleteButtonGroup.setVisible(false);

                        for(int i=0; i<groups.groups.length; i++)
                        groups.form.checkBox[i].setSelected(false);

                }//end if
                else if(index == 1)
                        {
                        checkAllGroup.setVisible(true);
                        addButtonGroup.setVisible(true);
                        addGroupContactButton.setVisible(true);
                        showAllButtonGroup.setVisible(true);
                        deleteButtonGroup.setVisible(true);
                        checkAll.setVisible(false);
                        addButton.setVisible(false);
                        addContactButton.setVisible(false);
                        deleteButton.setVisible(false);

                        for(int i=0; i<contacts.contacts.length; i++)
                        contacts.form.checkBox[i].setSelected(false);
                }//end if else
            }
        };

                        pane.addChangeListener(changeListener);

                        contactsPanel.setSize(100, 100);
```

```
                    contactsPanel.add( contactsTitle, BorderLayout.NORTH
);

                    contactsPanel.add( pane, BorderLayout.CENTER );
                    contactsPanel.add( buttonPanel, BorderLayout.SOUTH
);


                    container.add( messagePanel, BorderLayout.WEST );
                    container.add( contactsPanel, BorderLayout.CENTER );

                    setSize( 780, 347 );
            setVisible( true );

                }// end constructor

            public void paint( Graphics g )
            {
                    //call superclass's paint method
                    super.paint( g );

                    g.setColor( new Color(208, 224, 240) );
                    g.drawRect( 10, 50, 287, 270);
                    g.drawLine( 318, 49, 450, 49);
                    g.drawLine( 470, 49, 550, 49);
                    g.drawLine( 570, 49, 630, 49);
                    g.drawLine( 650, 49, 690, 49);
                    g.drawLine( 710, 49, 730, 49);

                    g.setColor( new Color(0, 0, 144) );
        //          g.drawLine( 305, 50, 305, 320);
                    g.drawLine( 307, 50, 307, 320);
                            }//end paint

}// end class FinalTest
```

3. AddContact.java

```
/* This class adds a new contact */
import java.awt.*;
import java.awt.event.*;
import javax.swing.*;
import javax.swing.text.*;
import java.io.*;
import java.text.*;
import javax.swing.JOptionPane;
import java.util.StringTokenizer;

public class AddContact extends JFrame {

        private String fileName, fileName2;
        private String firstName, secondName;
        JFrame frame = this;

    public AddContact (String name) {

        super("Add Details");
```

203

```java
        Object newSettings[] = {"Button.background", new Color(208,
224, 240),
                                        "Button.foreground", new
Color(0, 0, 144),
                                        "Panel.background", new
Color(255, 255, 255),
                                        "CheckBox.background",
new Color(255, 255, 255),
                                        "CheckBox.foreground",
new Color(0, 0, 144),
                                        "Label.foreground", new
Color(0, 0, 144), "Label.font",
                                        new Font("SansSerif",
Font.PLAIN, 14)
        };
        UIDefaults defaults = UIManager.getDefaults();
        defaults.putDefaults(newSettings);

        fileName = name + ".txt";
        fileName2 = name;

        String[] labels = { "First Name", "Last Name", "Mobile No.
+", "Email

        Address" };

        final TextForm form = new TextForm(labels);

        //Add a title label
        JLabel title = new JLabel("Add Contact",
SwingConstants.CENTER);
  title.setFont(new Font( "Serif", Font.BOLD, 20));

        // A button that adds new contact details to text.txt file
        JButton addbutton = new JButton("Add Contact");
        addbutton.addActionListener(new ActionListener() {
                        public void actionPerformed(ActionEvent
actionevent)
        {
        try {

                int countblanks = 0;
                for(int i=0; i<4; i++){
                        if( form.getEnteredText(i).equals(""))
                                countblanks++;
                }//end for

                if( countblanks != 0 )
                {
                        JOptionPane.showMessageDialog(null, "All
fields are required",
                                                                ""
,
JOptionPane.WARNING_MESSAGE );
```

204

```java
                }
                else
                {
                        boolean non_numeric_exists = false;
                        boolean email_exists = false;

                        // validate the Mobile No. field
                        // Ref: modified code accessed from:
                                                //
http://javaalmanac.com/egs/java.text/pkg.html
                        CharacterIterator no =
                                                        new
StringCharacterIterator(form.getEnteredText(2));
                                                // Iterate over the
characters in the forward direction
                                                for (char ch=no.first(); ch
!= CharacterIterator.DONE;

        ch=no.next()) {
                                                                if
(Character.isDigit(no.current())==false)
                                                                {

        non_numeric_exists = true;
                                                                }
                                                }

                                        //validate the email field
                                // Ref: modified code accessed from:
                                                //
http://javaalmanac.com/egs/java.text/pkg.html
                        CharacterIterator em =

        new StringCharacterIterator(form.getEnteredText(3));
                                                // Iterate over the
characters in the forward direction
                                                for (char ch=em.first(); ch
!= CharacterIterator.DONE;

                        ch=em.next()) {
                                                                if
(em.current()=='@')
                                                                {

        email_exists = true;
                                                                }
                                                }

                                if (non_numeric_exists)
                                {

        JOptionPane.showMessageDialog(null, "Only numeric data can
be
```

205

```
                        entered into the Mobile No. field.\nPlease try again",
                                                                   "",
JOptionPane.WARNING_MESSAGE );
                                    }

                        if (email_exists == false)
                        {

            JOptionPane.showMessageDialog(null, "Please enter a valid
Email

                Address\nFor example: emailaddress@hotmail.com",
                                                                   "",
JOptionPane.WARNING_MESSAGE );
                                    }

                        if (email_exists && non_numeric_exists ==
false)
                            {

                                FileWriter writer = new FileWriter(
fileName, true);

                                    // Create the buffered
reader for reading the file

            BufferedReader inFile = new BufferedReader(new FileReader(

                    fileName ));

                                    // Get the first line of the file
                                    String line =
inFile.readLine();

                                        boolean contactExists =
false;

                        int countcontacts = 0;

                        while ( line != null )
                            {
                                        // Create a
StringTokenizer with a "|" as a delimiter
                                        StringTokenizer st = new
StringTokenizer( line, "|" );

                                            //read first record

            secondName = st.nextToken();

            firstName = st.nextToken();
```

```java
        contactExists = ( firstName.equals(form.getEnteredText(0))
                                    &&
secondName.equals(form.getEnteredText(1)));
                                            if (contactExists
== true)

        countcontacts++;

                                        // process
remaining records
                                        line =
inFile.readLine();
                                }

                        if(countcontacts == 0)
                                {
                                    if(
form.getEnteredText(0).equals("") == false &&

            form.getEnteredText(1).equals("") == false &&

            form.getEnteredText(2).equals("") == false &&

            form.getEnteredText(3).equals("") == false )
                                            {
        PrintWriter pw = new PrintWriter( writer, true);

        pw.println( form.getEnteredText(1) + "|" +

                            form.getEnteredText(0) + "|+"

                            + form.getEnteredText(2) + "|" +

                            form.getEnteredText(3));

        pw.flush();
                                        pw.close();
                                        }
                                        else
                                        {
        JOptionPane.showMessageDialog(null, "All fields are
                        required", "",
JOptionPane.WARNING_MESSAGE );
                                                }
                                }
                        else
                            {
                                int n =
JOptionPane.showConfirmDialog(frame, "The Firstname
```

```java
                              and Lastname has been entered
        before..\nWould you like
                              to add the contact anyway?", "Duplicates
        Exist",
                              JOptionPane.YES_NO_OPTION);
                                             if (n ==
        JOptionPane.YES_OPTION) {

                PrintWriter pw = new PrintWriter( writer, true);
                pw.println( form.getEnteredText(1) + "|" +
                        form.getEnteredText(0) + "|+"
                        + form.getEnteredText(2) + "|" +
                        form.getEnteredText(3));
                pw.flush();
                                                     pw.close();
                        }

        }//end else
                                           } //end outer if
                        } //end outer else
                                } catch (IOException exception) {
                                System.out.println("Error adding contact");
                                exception.printStackTrace();
                                }
                        for(int i=0; i<4; i++)
                        form.resetText(i);

        }
                                });
                JButton clearbutton = new JButton( "Clear" );
                clearbutton.addActionListener(new ActionListener() {

                public void actionPerformed(ActionEvent actionevent)
        {
                for(int i=0; i<4; i++)
                        form.resetText(i);
        }

        });

                //A button to close the window
                        JButton closebutton = new JButton( "Close" );
                closebutton.addActionListener(new ActionListener() {

                public void actionPerformed(ActionEvent actionevent)
        {
                setVisible(false);

                if(fileName.equals("contacts.txt"))
                        {
                                FinalTest finaltest = new FinalTest();

                finaltest.setDefaultCloseOperation(JFrame.EXIT_ON_CLOSE );
                        }//end if
```

208

```
          else
               {
                    ShowGroupContacts showContacts = new
ShowGroupContacts(fileName2);

               showContacts.setDefaultCloseOperation(JFrame.EXIT_ON_CLO
SE );
                    }//end else
          }

          });

                    //create a button panel
                    JPanel buttonPanel = new JPanel();
                    buttonPanel.setLayout(new FlowLayout());
                    buttonPanel.add(addbutton);
                    buttonPanel.add(clearbutton);
                    buttonPanel.add(closebutton);

                    //layout
                    Container container = getContentPane();
                    container.setLayout(new BorderLayout());
                    container.setBackground(new Color(208, 224, 240));
                    container.add(title, BorderLayout.NORTH);
                    container.add(form, BorderLayout.CENTER);
                    container.add(buttonPanel, BorderLayout.SOUTH);
                    pack();
                    setVisible(true);

     }//end constructor

}//end class
```

4. TextForm.java

```
import javax.swing.*;
import java.awt.event.*;
import java.awt.*;

// A simple label/field form panel
public class TextForm extends JPanel {

          private JTextField[] textfield;
          //Create a form
          public TextForm(String[] labels) {
                    textfield = new JTextField[labels.length];
                    //Define layout
                    setLayout(new GridBagLayout());
                    setBackground(new Color(255, 255, 255));
                    GridBagConstraints constraints = new
GridBagConstraints();
                    constraints.anchor = GridBagConstraints.WEST;
                    constraints.insets = new Insets(2,2,2,2);
```

```java
            //Add labels and fields as specified
            for(int i=0; i<labels.length; i++) {
                    JLabel label = new JLabel(labels[i]);
                    label.setFont(new Font("SansSerif",
Font.PLAIN, 14));
                    label.setForeground(new Color(0, 0, 144));
                    textfield[i] = new JTextField( 15 );
                    label.setLabelFor(textfield[i]);
// sets accessibleName for  textfield[i]
                    //layout labels and fields
                    constraints.gridy = i;
                    constraints.gridx = 0;
                    add(label, constraints);
                    constraints.gridx = 1;
                    add(textfield[i], constraints);
            }// end for
    }//end constructor

    //Set the contents of one of the textfields
    public void resetText(int index) {
            textfield[index].setText("");
    }// end method getEnteredText

    //Get the contents of one of the textfields
    public String getEnteredText(int index) {
            return textfield[index].getText();
    }// end method getEnteredText
}
```

5. DisplayContacts.java

```
/* This class reads the mobile number, first name, last name and email
address
from a contacts file contacts.txt into an array of Contact
objects.  insertion sort is used to sort the
contacts information in alphabetical order of lastname.  The contact
information
is sorted starting with lastnames beginning with "A" */

import java.awt.*;
import java.awt.event.*;
import javax.swing.*;
import java.io.*;
import java.util.StringTokenizer;

public class DisplayContacts  extends JPanel {

        static int contactCount;
        public static Contact contacts[];
        public static DisplayTextForm form;

        public DisplayContacts (String groupfilename) {

                String groupFileName = groupfilename + ".txt";
                File contactFile = new File( groupFileName );
                String firstName, secondName, MobileNum,
emailAddress;

        // Make sure that the file contacts.txt exists and has
        // valid data records.  Otherwise, exceptions will occur.
        if ( contactFile.exists() )
                    {
                            int count = 0;

                            try {

                                    /*count the number of contacts in
the list so as to
                                    find out how big to make the
array.*/
                                    // Create the buffered reader for
reading the file
                                    BufferedReader infile = new
BufferedReader(new FileReader(

                contactFile ));

                                    // Get the first line of the file
                        String aline = infile.readLine();

                                    while(aline!=null) {
                                            aline=infile.readLine();
```

```java
                                        count=count+1;
                                    }//end while

                                    // Close the BufferedReader
                    infile.close();

                        }// end try
                    catch (IOException e) {
            System.err.println("Error: " + e);
                    }

                        try {
                                    // Create the buffered reader for
reading the file
                                    BufferedReader inFile = new
BufferedReader(new FileReader(

                                    contactFile ));

                                    // Get the first line of the file
                    String line = inFile.readLine();

                                    //create a new array of Student
objects
                                        contacts = new Contact[count];

                                    // process all the contact records
                    contactCount = 0;

                                    while ( line != null )
                        {
                                    // Create a StringTokenizer with a "|" as a
delimiter
                    StringTokenizer st = new StringTokenizer( line, "|" );

                                            //read first record
                                            secondName =
st.nextToken();

                                            firstName = st.nextToken();
                                            MobileNum =
st.nextToken();

                                            emailAddress =
st.nextToken();

                                            // call the Contact
constructor
                    contacts[contactCount] = new Contact(secondName,
firstName,

                    MobileNum, emailAddress);

                                    // process remaining records
                                    line=inFile.readLine();
```

```java
                    contactCount++;

            }//end while

                            // Close the BufferedReader
            inFile.close();

                            Sorts.insertionSort(contacts);

                            String name[] = new
String[contacts.length];
                            String mobile[] = new
String[contacts.length];
                            String email[] = new
String[contacts.length];

                            //dump to standard output
                            for(int i=0; i<contacts.length; i++)
{
                                    name[i] =
contacts[i].getName();
                                    mobile[i] =
contacts[i].getMobileNum();
                                    email[i] =
contacts[i].getEmail();
                            }

                            form = new DisplayTextForm(name,
mobile, email);
                            //layout
                            this.setLayout(new BorderLayout());

                            JScrollPane pane = new
JScrollPane(form);
                            pane.setBackground(new Color(208,
224, 240));
                add(pane, BorderLayout.CENTER);
                                            } // end try
                catch (IOException e) {
            System.err.println("Error: " + e);
                }

            }//end if
            else
                        System.out.println("File does not exist in
current directory");

        }// end constructor

}//end class DisplayContacts
```

6. Contact.java

213

```java
/*This class can be used to represent contacts namely:
First Name, last Name, Mobile No. and Email Address.
Methods to access the attributes are also provided */

public class Contact implements Comparable {
        private String mobileNum, firstName, lastName, email;


        //Contact constructor
        public Contact (String lName, String fName, String
mNum, String eAdd){
                mobileNum = mNum;
                firstName = fName;
                lastName = lName;
                email = eAdd;
        }//end Contact constructor

        //accessor for mobileNum
        public String getMobileNum() {
                return mobileNum + "    ";
        }

        //accessor for mobileNum
        public String getMobileNumPlain() {
                return mobileNum;
        }

        //accessor for mobileNum
        public String getMobileNumComma() {
                return mobileNum + ",";
        }

        //accessor for firstName
        public String getFirstName () {
                return firstName;
        }

        //accessor for lastName
        public String getLastName () {
                return lastName;
        }

        //accessor for email
        public String getEmail () {
                return email;
        }

        public String getName() {
                return lastName + ", " + firstName + "    ";
        }

        public String toString () {
```

```java
                    return lastName + ", " + firstName + "  " +
mobileNum + "  " + email;
                }

                // this method was taken from "Java Software
Solutions",
                // by: Lewis and Loftus, 2nd edition
                // May 2000, page 296.
                public int compareTo (Object other) {
                        int result;

                        if
(lastName.equals(((Contact)other).lastName))
                                result =
firstName.compareTo(((Contact)other).firstName);
                        else
                                result =
lastName.compareTo(((Contact)other).lastName);

                        return result;
                }

}//end Contact class
```

7. Sorts.java

```java
//this class was taken from "Java Software Solutions", by: Lewis and
Loftus, 2nd edition
//May 2000, pages 290-295
public class Sorts {

        // Sorts the specified array of objects using the insertion
        //sort algorithm
        public static void insertionSort (Comparable[] objects) {
                for(int index = 1; index<objects.length; index++) {
                        Comparable key = objects[index];
                        int position = index;
                        // Shift larger values to the right
                        while (position>0 && objects[position-
1].compareTo(key) > 0) {
                                objects[position] = objects[position-
1];

                                position--;
                        }

                        objects[position] = key;

                }
        }

}
```

8. DisplayTextForm.java

```java
import javax.swing.*;
import java.awt.event.*;
import java.awt.*;

// A simple label/field form panel
public class DisplayTextForm extends JPanel {

        public JCheckBox[] checkBox;
        //Create a form

public DisplayTextForm(String[] names, String[] mobiles, String[]
emails) {
Object newSettings[] = {"Button.background", new Color(208, 224,
240),
"Button.foreground", new Color(0, 0, 144), "Panel.background",
new Color(255, 255, 255),
"CheckBox.font", new Font("SansSerif", Font.PLAIN, 12),
"CheckBox.background", new Color(255, 255, 255),
"CheckBox.foreground", new Color(0, 0, 144),
"Label.foreground", new Color(0, 0, 144), "Label.font",
new Font("SansSerif", Font.PLAIN, 12)
                };
                UIDefaults defaults = UIManager.getDefaults();
                defaults.putDefaults(newSettings);
                checkBox = new JCheckBox[names.length];
                //Define layout
                FlowLayout layout = new FlowLayout();
                setLayout(layout);
                layout.setAlignment( FlowLayout.LEFT );
                JPanel panel = new JPanel();//
                panel.setLayout(new GridBagLayout());
                GridBagConstraints constraints = new
GridBagConstraints();
                constraints.anchor = GridBagConstraints.WEST;
                constraints.insets = new Insets(0,0,0,0);

                //Add labels and fields as specified
                for(int i=0; i<names.length; i++) {
                        String name = names[i];
                        JLabel mobile = new JLabel(mobiles[i]);
                        JLabel email = new JLabel(emails[i]);

                        checkBox[i] = new JCheckBox(name);
                        checkBox[i].setSelected(false);

                        //layout labels and fields
                        constraints.gridy = i; //rows
                        constraints.gridx = 0; //columns
                        panel.add(checkBox[i], constraints);
                        constraints.gridx = 1;
                        panel.add(mobile, constraints);
                        constraints.gridx = 2;
```

```java
                    panel.add(email, constraints);
            }// end for

            add(panel);
    }//end constructor

    public void paint( Graphics g )
    {
            //call superclass's paint method
            super.paint( g );

            g.setColor( new Color(208, 224, 240) );
            for(int x=0,y=30; x<checkBox.length; x++,y+=25){
                    g.drawLine( 5, y, 430, y);
            }//end for
    }//end paint

}//end class
```

9. AddGroup.java

```java
import java.awt.*;
import java.awt.event.*;
import javax.swing.*;
import java.text.*;
import javax.swing.text.*;
import java.io.*;
import java.util.StringTokenizer;

public class AddGroup extends JFrame {

        private File groupFile;

  public AddGroup () {

        super("Add Group Details");

        Object newSettings[] = {"Button.background", new Color(208,
224, 240),
                              "Button.foreground", new Color(0, 0,
144),
                              "Panel.background", new Color(255,
255, 255),
                              "CheckBox.background", new
Color(255, 255, 255),
                              "CheckBox.foreground", new
Color(0, 0, 144),
                              "Label.foreground", new Color(0, 0,
144), "Label.font",
                              new Font("SansSerif", Font.PLAIN,
14)
        };
        UIDefaults defaults = UIManager.getDefaults();
        defaults.putDefaults(newSettings);

        groupFile = new File( "groups.txt" );

        String[] labels = { "Group Name", "First Name", "Last Name",
"Mobile No.
        +", "Email Address" };

        final TextForm form = new TextForm(labels);

        //Add a title label
        JLabel title;
        title = new JLabel("Create/Add To Group",
SwingConstants.CENTER);
        title.setFont(new Font( "Serif", Font.BOLD, 20));

        // A button that adds new contact details to groups.txt file
        JButton addbutton = new JButton("Add Contact");
        addbutton.addActionListener(new ActionListener() {
```

```java
                    public void actionPerformed(ActionEvent
actionevent)
        {
        try {

            FileWriter writer = new FileWriter( "groups.txt", true);

            // Create the buffered reader for reading the file
                        BufferedReader inFile = new
BufferedReader(new FileReader(


                                                        groupFile
));

                String line = inFile.readLine();

            boolean groupExists = false;
            int countgroups = 0;

            while (line != null)
            {

                groupExists = (
line.equals(form.getEnteredText(0)));
                if (groupExists == true)
                        countgroups++;

                line = inFile.readLine();

            }

            if(countgroups == 0)
            {
                if( form.getEnteredText(0).equals("") ==
false )
                {
                        PrintWriter pw = new PrintWriter(
writer, true);

                        pw.println( form.getEnteredText(0));
                        pw.flush();
                        pw.close();
                }//end inner if
            }

            if( form.getEnteredText(0).equals("") == false )
            {
                String groupName =
form.getEnteredText(0) + ".txt";
                                        FileWriter
writer2 = new FileWriter( groupName, true);
                    PrintWriter pw2 = new PrintWriter(
writer2, true);
```

220

```java
                                    int countblanks = 0;
                                    for(int i=1; i<5; i++){
                                        if(
form.getEnteredText(i).equals(""))
                                                    countblanks++;
                                    }//end for

                                    if( countblanks < 4 && countblanks
> 0 )
                                        {

            JOptionPane.showMessageDialog(null, "All fields are required

            in order to add a contact to the group.",
                                                                    "",
JOptionPane.WARNING_MESSAGE );
                                        }

                                    if( countblanks == 0 )
                                        {

                                            boolean non_numeric_exists
= false;
                                            boolean email_exists =
false;

                                            //validate the Mobile No.
field
                                            // Ref: modified code
accessed from:

        // http://javaalmanac.com/egs/java.text/pkg.html
                                            CharacterIterator no =

            new StringCharacterIterator(form.getEnteredText(3));
                                                    // Iterate
over the characters in the forward direction
                                                        for (char
ch=no.first(); ch != CharacterIterator.DONE;

                                            ch=no.next()) {
                                                                    if
(Character.isDigit(no.current())==false)
                                                                        {

            non_numeric_exists = true;
                                                                        }
                                                    }
CharacterIterator em = new
StringCharacterIterator(form.getEnteredText(4));
Iterate over the characters in the forward direction
    for (char ch=em.first(); ch != CharacterIterator.DONE;
        ch=em.next()) {
        if (em.current()=='@')
```

```java
                    {
                    email_exists = true;
                    }
                                                            }
                                                                        if
(non_numeric_exists)
                        {

        JOptionPane.showMessageDialog(null, "Only numeric data can
        be entered into the Mobile No. field.\nPlease try again", "",
JOptionPane.WARNING_MESSAGE );
                                                    }

                                        if (email_exists == false)
                                        {

        JOptionPane.showMessageDialog(null, "Please enter a valid

                        Email Address\nFor example:
emailaddress@hotmail.com",

        "", JOptionPane.WARNING_MESSAGE );
                                                    }

                                        if (email_exists &&
non_numeric_exists == false)
                                        {
                                                    pw2.println (
form.getEnteredText(2) + "|" +

                        form.getEnteredText(1) + "|+" +
form.getEnteredText(3)

                                + "|" + form.getEnteredText(4));
                                                    }//end if
                                        }
                                        pw2.flush();
                                        pw2.close();
                        }
            } catch (IOException exception) {
                                System.out.println("Error adding contact");
                                exception.printStackTrace();
                                }
                        for(int i=1; i<5; i++)
                        form.resetText(i);
            }

                        });
                        //A button to reset the textfields
                        JButton clearbutton = new JButton( "Clear" );
                        clearbutton.addActionListener(new ActionListener() {

            public void actionPerformed(ActionEvent actionevent)
    {
            for(int i=0; i<5; i++)
```

```java
            form.resetText(i);
    }

    });
                //A button to close the window
                JButton closebutton = new JButton( "Close" );
                closebutton.addActionListener(new ActionListener() {

    public void actionPerformed(ActionEvent actionevent)
    {
        setVisible(false);
        FinalTest finaltest = new FinalTest();

        finaltest.setDefaultCloseOperation(JFrame.EXIT_ON_CLOSE );
    }
    });
                //create a button panel
                JPanel buttonPanel = new JPanel();
                buttonPanel.setLayout(new FlowLayout());
                buttonPanel.add(addbutton);
                buttonPanel.add(clearbutton);
                buttonPanel.add(closebutton);

                //layout
                Container container = getContentPane();
                container.setLayout(new BorderLayout());
                container.setBackground(new Color(208, 224, 240));
                container.add(title, BorderLayout.NORTH);
                container.add(form, BorderLayout.CENTER);
                container.add(buttonPanel, BorderLayout.SOUTH);
                pack();
                setVisible(true);

    }//end constructor

}//end class
```

10. DisplayTheGroups.java

```java
import java.awt.*;
import java.awt.event.*;
import javax.swing.*;
import javax.swing.text.*;
import java.io.*;
import java.util.StringTokenizer;

public class DisplayTheGroups extends JPanel {

        static int groupCount;
        public static Group groups[];
        public static DisplayGroups form;

        public DisplayTheGroups () {

                File groupFile = new File( "groups.txt" );
                String groupName;

    // Make sure that the file groups.txt exists and has
    // valid data records.  Otherwise, exceptions will occur.
    if ( groupFile.exists() )
                {
                        int count = 0;

                        try {

                                /*count the number of groups in the
list so as to
                                find out how big to make the
array.*/
                                // Create the buffered reader for
reading the file
                                BufferedReader infile = new
BufferedReader(new FileReader(


                                                                groupFile
));

                                // Get the first line of the file
                String aline = infile.readLine();

                                while(aline!=null) {
                                        aline=infile.readLine();
                                        count=count+1;
                                }//end while

                                // Close the BufferedReader
                infile.close();

                        }// end try
                catch (IOException e) {
```

```java
            System.err.println("Error: " + e);
            }

            try {
                        // Create the buffered reader for
reading the file
                        BufferedReader inFile = new
BufferedReader(new FileReader(

                                                                        groupFile
));
                        // Get the first line of the file
            String line = inFile.readLine();

            //create a new array of Group objects
                        groups = new Group[count];

                        // process all the contact records
            groupCount = 0;

                        while ( line != null )
            {
                        // Create a StringTokenizer with a "|" as a
delimiter
            StringTokenizer st = new StringTokenizer( line );

                                    //read first record
                                    groupName =
st.nextToken();

                                    // call the Contact
constructor
            groups[groupCount] = new Group(groupName);

                        // process remaining records
            line=inFile.readLine();

            groupCount++;

            }//end while

                        // Close the BufferedReader
            inFile.close();

                        // this method was taken from "Java
Software Solutions",

                        // by: Lewis and Loftus, 2nd edition
                        // May 2000, page 296.
            Sorts.insertionSort(groups);

            String name[] = new
String[groups.length];
```

225

```java
                                    //dump to standard output
                                    for(int i=0; i<groups.length; i++)
                                            name[i] =
groups[i].getName();


                                    form = new DisplayGroups(name);

                                    //layout
                                    this.setLayout(new BorderLayout());

                                    JScrollPane pane = new
JScrollPane(form);

                                    add(pane, BorderLayout.CENTER);

                    } // end try
              catch (IOException e) {
        System.err.println("Error: " + e);
              }

              }//end if
              else
                      System.out.println("File does not exist in
current directory");

        }// end constructor

}//end class DisplayTheGroups
```

11. Group.java

```java
public class Group implements Comparable {
        private String name;

        //Group constructor
        public Group (String gname){
                name = gname;
        }//end Group constructor

        //accessor for name
        public String getName() {
                return name;
        }

        //this method was taken from "Java Software
Solutions",
        //by: Lewis and Loftus, 2nd edition
        //May 2000, page 296.
        public int compareTo (Object other) {
                int result;

                result =
name.compareTo(((Group)other).name);

                return result;
        }

}//end Group class
```

12. DisplayGroups.java

```java
import javax.swing.*;
import java.awt.event.*;
import java.awt.*;

// A simple label/field form panel
public class DisplayGroups extends JPanel {

        public JCheckBox[] checkBox;
        //Create a form

        public DisplayGroups(String[] names) {

                Object newSettings[] = {"Button.background", new
Color(208, 224, 240),
                                        "Button.foreground", new
Color(0, 0, 144),
                                        "Panel.background", new
Color(255, 255, 255),
                                        "CheckBox.font", new
Font("SansSerif", Font.PLAIN, 12),
                                        "CheckBox.background",
new Color(255, 255, 255),
                                        "CheckBox.foreground",
new Color(0, 0, 144),
                                        "Label.foreground", new
Color(0, 0, 144), "Label.font",
                                        new Font("SansSerif",
Font.PLAIN, 14)
                };
                UIDefaults defaults = UIManager.getDefaults();
                defaults.putDefaults(newSettings);

                checkBox = new JCheckBox[names.length];

                //Define layout
                FlowLayout layout = new FlowLayout();
                setLayout(layout);
                layout.setAlignment( FlowLayout.LEFT );

                JPanel panel = new JPanel();
                panel.setLayout(new GridBagLayout());

                GridBagConstraints constraints = new
GridBagConstraints();
                constraints.anchor = GridBagConstraints.WEST;
                constraints.insets = new Insets(0,0,0,0);

                //Add labels and fields as specified
                for(int i=0; i<names.length; i++) {
                        String name = names[i];

                        checkBox[i] = new JCheckBox(name);
```

```java
                        checkBox[i].setSelected(false);

                        //layout labels and fields
                        constraints.gridy = i; //rows
                        constraints.gridx = 0; //columns
                        panel.add(checkBox[i], constraints);//

                }// end for

                add(panel);
        }//end constructor

        public void paint( Graphics g )
        {
                //call superclass's paint method
                super.paint( g );

                g.setColor( new Color(208, 224, 240) );
                for(int x=0,y=30; x<checkBox.length; x++,y+=25){
                        g.drawLine( 5, y, 430, y);
                }//end for
        }//end paint

}//end class
```

13. GatherGroupContacts.java

```
/* This class reads the mobile number, first name, last name and email
address from a contacts file contacts.txt into an array of Contact
objects.  insertion sort is used to sort the contacts information in
alphabetical order of lastname.  The contact information
is sorted starting with lastnames beginning with "A" */

import java.awt.*;
import java.awt.event.*;
import javax.swing.*;
import java.io.*;
import java.util.StringTokenizer;

public class GatherGroupContacts {

        static int contactCount;
        public static Contact contacts[];

        public GatherGroupContacts (String groupname) {

                String fileName = groupname + ".txt";
                File contactFile = new File( fileName );
                String firstName, secondName, MobileNum,
emailAddress;

        // Make sure that the file contacts.txt exists and has
        // valid data records.  Otherwise, exceptions will occur.
        if ( contactFile.exists() )
                {
                        int count = 0;

                        try {

                                /*count the number of contacts in
the list so as to
                                find out how big to make the
array.*/
                                // Create the buffered reader for
reading the file
                                BufferedReader infile = new
BufferedReader(new FileReader(


                                                            contactFile
));

                                // Get the first line of the file
                        String aline = infile.readLine();

                                while(aline!=null) {
                                        aline=infile.readLine();
                                        count=count+1;
                                }//end while
```

```java
                                    // Close the BufferedReader
                    infile.close();

                        }// end try
                catch (IOException e) {
            System.err.println("Error: " + e);
                }

                    try {
                                // Create the buffered reader for
reading the file
                                BufferedReader inFile = new
BufferedReader(new FileReader(


                                                        contactFile
));
                                // Get the first line of the file
                    String line = inFile.readLine();

                                //create a new array of Student
objects
                                contacts = new Contact[count];

                                // process all the contact records
                    contactCount = 0;

                        while ( line != null )
            {
                            // Create a StringTokenizer with a "|" as a
delimiter
            StringTokenizer st = new StringTokenizer( line, "|" );

                                    //read first record
                                    secondName =
st.nextToken();
                                    firstName = st.nextToken();
                                    MobileNum =
st.nextToken();
                                    emailAddress =
st.nextToken();

                                    // call the Contact
constructor
                    contacts[contactCount] = new Contact(secondName,
firstName,


                                    MobileNum, emailAddress);

                        // process remaining records
                        line=inFile.readLine();
```

```java
                    contactCount++;

        }//end while

                                // Close the BufferedReader
            inFile.close();

                                //this method was taken from "Java
Software Solutions",

                                //by: Lewis and Loftus, 2nd edition
                                //May 2000, page 296.
                                Sorts.insertionSort(contacts);

                } // end try
            catch (IOException e) {
        System.err.println("Error: " + e);
                }

            }//end if
            else
                        System.out.println("File does not exist in
current directory");

        }// end constructor

}//end class GatherGroupContacts
```

14. ShowGroupContacts.java

```java
import java.awt.*;
import java.awt.event.*;
import javax.swing.*;
import javax.swing.text.*;
import java.io.*;
import java.util.StringTokenizer;

public class ShowGroupContacts extends JFrame {

        private String fileName, name;
        private DisplayContacts contacts;

  public ShowGroupContacts (String groupfilename) {

            super("Group Details");

            Object newSettings[] = {"Button.background", new
Color(208, 224, 240),
                        "Button.foreground", new Color(0, 0,
144),
                        "Panel.background", new Color(255,
255, 255),
                        "CheckBox.font", new
Font("SansSerif", Font.PLAIN, 12),
                        "CheckBox.background", new
Color(255, 255, 255),
                        "CheckBox.foreground", new
Color(0, 0, 144),
                        "Label.foreground", new Color(0, 0,
144), "Label.font",
                        new Font("SansSerif", Font.PLAIN,
14)
            };
            UIDefaults defaults = UIManager.getDefaults();
            defaults.putDefaults(newSettings);

            fileName = groupfilename;
            name = groupfilename + ".txt";
            contacts = new DisplayContacts (groupfilename);

            //Add a title label
            String header = "  " + groupfilename;
            JLabel title;
            title = new JLabel(header, SwingConstants.LEFT);
            title.setFont(new Font( "Serif", Font.BOLD, 20));

            // A button that adds new contact details to the group
file
            JButton addbutton = new JButton("Add Contact");
            addbutton.addActionListener(new ActionListener() {
                    public void actionPerformed(ActionEvent
actionevent)
```

```java
                {
            AddContact addcontact = new AddContact(fileName);

            addcontact.setDefaultCloseOperation(JFrame.HIDE_ON_CLOSE
);

            setVisible( false );

        }

                });

                JButton deleteButton = new JButton("Delete");
                deleteButton.addActionListener(new ActionListener() {
            public void actionPerformed(ActionEvent actionevent)
        {
            try {
                FileWriter writer = new FileWriter( name, false);
                                PrintWriter pw = new
PrintWriter( writer, true);

                for(int i=0; i<contacts.contacts.length; i++) {

        if(contacts.form.checkBox[i].isSelected()==false) {
                                pw.println(
contacts.contacts[i].getLastName() + "|" +

                contacts.contacts[i].getFirstName() + "|"

                + contacts.contacts[i].getMobileNumPlain() + "|" +

                contacts.contacts[i].getEmail());
                        }//end if
                } //end for
                pw.flush();
                pw.close();
        } catch (IOException exception) {
                System.out.println("Error adding contact");
                        exception.printStackTrace();
                        } //end catch

            setVisible( false );

            ShowGroupContacts showContacts = new
ShowGroupContacts(fileName);

            showContacts.setDefaultCloseOperation(JFrame.HIDE_ON_CLO
SE );
        }
                });

                //A button to close the window
```

```java
            JButton closebutton = new JButton( "Close" );
            closebutton.addActionListener(new ActionListener() {

    public void actionPerformed(ActionEvent actionevent)
{
    setVisible(false);
}

            });

            //create a button panel
            JPanel buttonPanel = new JPanel();
            FlowLayout buttonLayout = new FlowLayout();
            buttonLayout.setAlignment( FlowLayout.LEFT );
            buttonPanel.setLayout(buttonLayout);
            buttonPanel.add(addbutton);
            buttonPanel.add(closebutton);
            buttonPanel.add(deleteButton);

            //layout
            Container container = getContentPane();
            container.setLayout(new BorderLayout());
            container.setBackground(new Color(208, 224, 240));
            container.add(title, BorderLayout.NORTH);
            container.add(contacts, BorderLayout.CENTER);
            container.add(buttonPanel, BorderLayout.SOUTH);
            setSize(460, 295);
            setVisible(true);

    }//end constructor

}//end class
```

15. Implementation.java

```java
//the entire application
import java.awt.*;
import java.awt.event.*;
import javax.swing.*;
import java.io.*;

public class Implementation
{

        // execute application
    public static void main( String args[] )
    {
                    File subscriberFile = new File( "subscriber.ini" );

                    if ( subscriberFile.exists() )
                    {
                            FinalTest finaltest = new FinalTest();

            finaltest.setDefaultCloseOperation(JFrame.EXIT_ON_CLOSE );

                    }
                    else {
                            Id_Password idpass = new Id_Password();

            idpass.setDefaultCloseOperation(JFrame.EXIT_ON_CLOSE );
                    }

    }

}
```

16. Id_Password.java

```java
/* This class sets the Subscriber Id and Password */
import java.awt.*;
import java.awt.event.*;
import javax.swing.*;
import javax.swing.text.*;
import java.io.*;
import javax.swing.JOptionPane;

public class Id_Password extends JFrame {

        JFrame frame = this;

  public Id_Password () {

                super("Subscriber Id & Password");

                Object newSettings[] = {"Button.background", new
Color(208, 224, 240),
                        "Button.foreground", new Color(0, 0,
144),
                        "Panel.background", new Color(255,
255, 255),
                        "CheckBox.font", new
Font("SansSerif", Font.PLAIN, 12),
                        "CheckBox.background", new
Color(255, 255, 255),
                        "CheckBox.foreground", new
Color(0, 0, 144),
                        "Label.foreground", new Color(0, 0,
144), "Label.font",
                        new Font("SansSerif", Font.PLAIN,
12),
                        "OptionPane.background", new
Color(255, 255, 255),
                        "OptionPane.messageForeground",
new Color(0, 0, 144),
                        "ScrollBar.background", new
Color(255, 255, 255)
                };
                UIDefaults defaults = UIManager.getDefaults();
                defaults.putDefaults(newSettings);

                String[] labels = { "Subscriber Id:", "Subscriber
Password:" };

                final TextForm form = new TextForm(labels);

                //Add a title label
                JLabel title = new JLabel("Enter Subscriber Id &
Password",

                        SwingConstants.CENTER);
```

```java
        title.setFont(new Font( "Serif", Font.BOLD, 20));

                    // A button that creates and adds Subscriber Id and
Password to
                    // subscriber.ini file
                    JButton addbutton = new JButton("Ok");
                    addbutton.addActionListener(new ActionListener() {
                            public void actionPerformed(ActionEvent
actionevent)
            {
            try {

                    if ((form.getEnteredText(0).equals("814-814-814-
81473") &&

                    form.getEnteredText(1).equals("D26C7732"))==false) {

                            JOptionPane.showMessageDialog(null,
"Invalid Subscriber Id and
                                                            Password,
please try again.", "", JOptionPane.ERROR_MESSAGE );
                                    form.resetText(0);
                                    form.resetText(1);
                    }

                    else {       FileWriter writer = new FileWriter(
"subscriber.ini", false);
                            PrintWriter pw = new PrintWriter( writer,
true);
                                                            pw.println(
form.getEnteredText(0) );
                                    pw.println( form.getEnteredText(1) );
                                                            pw.flush();
                                    pw.close();

                                    setVisible(false);

                                    JOptionPane.showMessageDialog(null,
"Subscriber Id & Password has
                                                            been set
successfully!\nEnjoy using the SMS Messenger

            Application.", "", JOptionPane.INFORMATION_MESSAGE );

                                    FinalTest finaltest = new FinalTest();

            finaltest.setDefaultCloseOperation(JFrame.EXIT_ON_CLOSE );
                    }

            } catch (IOException exception) {
                            System.out.println("Error entering Subscriber
Id and Password");
```

```java
                    exception.printStackTrace();
                }

    }

        });

            //A button to close the window
            JButton closebutton = new JButton( "Close" );
        closebutton.addActionListener(new ActionListener() {

    public void actionPerformed(ActionEvent actionevent)
{
    System.exit(0);
}

        });

            //create a button panel
            JPanel buttonPanel = new JPanel();
            buttonPanel.setLayout(new FlowLayout());
            buttonPanel.add(addbutton);
            buttonPanel.add(closebutton);

            //layout
            Container container = getContentPane();
            container.setLayout(new BorderLayout());
            container.setBackground(new Color(208, 224, 240));
            container.add(title, BorderLayout.NORTH);
            container.add(form, BorderLayout.CENTER);
            container.add(buttonPanel, BorderLayout.SOUTH);
            pack();
            setVisible(true);

    }//end constructor

}//end class
```

Appendix K: Simplewire Wireless Messaging Platform Error Codes

The following error codes are used within the Simplewire™ Wireless Messaging Platform. Every error has an error code, error class, and description attached to it. An error code in the range of 100 - 300 is specifically reserved for client-side errors that differ among all SMS Software Development Kit versions. These errors are embedded in the SDK itself [Simplewire].

Code	Class	Error Description
0	Delivery	Message successfully sent to carrier.
1	Processing	Processing request.
2	Processing	Message successfully queued.
4	Delivery	Message successfully delivered.
302	Syntax	The xml document could not be validated.
321	Syntax	Invalid request version.
322	Syntax	Invalid request protocol.
330	Syntax	Invalid number of page elements.
331	Syntax	The message alias was invalid.
341	Syntax	The message service id does not exist.
342	Syntax	A message service id id is required.
343	Syntax	The message service id is discontinued.
344	Syntax	The message service id is beta.
345	Network	Unable to determine carrier id from pin.
350	Syntax	A message pin is required.
351	Syntax	The message pin is not long enough.
352	Syntax	The message pin is too long.
353	Syntax	Message text is required.
354	Syntax	Message text is not long enough.
355	Syntax	Message text is too long.
356	Syntax	Message from is required.
357	Syntax	Message from is not long enough.
358	Syntax	Message from is too long.
359	Syntax	Message callback is required.
360	Syntax	Message callback is not long enough.
361	Syntax	Message callback is too long.
380	Syntax	Invalid data coding scheme.
385	Syntax	Invalid or unsupported ringtone format.
386	Syntax	Invalid or unsupported image format.
388	Syntax	Smart messg not supported for this carrier.
389	Syntax	A valid image type must be specified.
390	Syntax	Must provide numeric network codes.
391	Syntax	Must provide ringtone data.
392	Syntax	Must provide Image data.
450	Account	Message account limit exceeded.
460	Account	ubscriber id not found within network.
500	Delivery	Carrier service temporarily unavailable.
501	Delivery	Carrier unknown subscriber.
502	Delivery	Carrier network time-out.

503	Delivery	Carrier facility not provided.
504	Delivery	Carrier call barred.
505	Delivery	Carrier operation barred.
506	Delivery	Carrier SC congestion.
507	Delivery	Carrier facility not supported.
508	Delivery	Carrier absent subscriber.
509	Delivery	Carrier delivery fail.
510	Delivery	Carrier protocol error.
511	Delivery	Carrier MS not equipped.
512	Delivery	Carrier unknown SC.
513	Delivery	Carrier illegal MS.
514	Delivery	Carrier MS not a subscriber.
515	Delivery	Carrier error in MS.
516	Delivery	Carrier SMS lower layer not provisioned.
517	Delivery	Carrier system fail.
518	Delivery	Carrier PLMN system failure.
519	Delivery	Carrier HLR system failure.
520	Delivery	Carrier VLR system failure.
521	Delivery	Carrier previous VLR system failure.
522	Delivery	Carrier controlling MSC system failure.
523	Delivery	Carrier VMSC system failure.
524	Delivery	Carrier EIR system failure.
525	Delivery	Carrier system failure.
526	Delivery	Carrier unexpected data value.
527	Delivery	Carrier error in address service center.
528	Delivery	Carrier invalid absolute validity period.
529	Delivery	Carrier short message exceeds maximum.
532	Delivery	Carrier invalid validity period format.
533	Delivery	Carrier invalid destination address.
534	Delivery	Carrier duplicate message submit.
600	Syntax	Carrier checksum error.
601	Syntax	Carrier syntax error.
602	Syntax	Carrier operation not supported by system.
603	Delivery	Carrier call barring active.
623	Delivery	Message not found.
624	Delivery	Subscriber hang-up.
625	Delivery	RPID already in use.
626	Delivery	Delivery in progress.
627	Delivery	Message forwarded.
701	Syntax	Message ticket id is required.
710	Syntax	Invalid ticket id format.
711	Processing ·	Ticket id does not exist within the network.
712	Syntax	Invalid ticket id since it was null.
802	Syntax	Service id is required.
803	Syntax	Invalid service id since it was null.
810	Delivery	Failed message delivery.
811	Delivery	Message validity period expired.
2001	Authentication	Invalid subscription authentication.
2002	Authentication	Subscriber id has been de-activated.
2003	Authentication	Subscriber id has been deleted.
4000	Syntax	The alias function has been deprecated.